Miracles at Midnight

Vignettes from Living on Mission

John Shackelford
edited by Phee Paradise

Miracles at Midnight

ISBN-13: 978-1-938092-75-6
ISBN-10: 1938092759

Published by Pix-N-Pens, 2631 Holly Springs Pkwy. Box 35, Holly Springs, GA 30142.

www.PixNPens.com

Printed in the United States of America.

Table of Contents

Preface

Dear Reader,

We have not written these stories to be deep theological discussions from an erudite scholar's reflections on theology but rather to be simple homespun stories of God at work in the lives of people. God has a marvelous way of using our weaknesses to magnify Himself in the day by day things that come our way. It is our hope that you will be blessed as you see what God has done in other people and lands.

We have been reluctant to write them down because they have become an autobiography and the use of the pronouns we, us and ours caused us to hesitate putting them on paper. These stories are much more than what happened to us; they are the stories of God doing His work and how events and circumstances in our lives were used by Him. We are grateful and humbled that He allowed us to be involved.

As John began to write stories for our grandchildren and family, Esther would edit them. As we discussed them and corrected the way they were recorded we realized that she was as deeply involved as John and that was when we decided that her stories had to be included also. As we looked at letters her mother had saved and related to days past, the whole picture came into focus. She just had to be included and so these vignettes include her times of testing, joys, and the miracles of God at work for both of us.

As you read, do give God the Praise and thank Him for leading and directing us.

Enjoy...

John and Esther

Dear Reader,

These are my father's stories. Before God called him home, I had the privilege of editing them for him. The stories are mostly about his work on the mission field, but there are some personal notes that may need a little explaining. John and Esther raised five children in Guatemala. You will see our names, Peggy (or Pep), Fred, Charlotte, Phyllis (or Phee) and Janet, but the stories aren't about us. Don't think that means the work was more important to them than their family. We were well loved and happy, raised to serve God ourselves. We truly have a rich heritage and we are the first to give God the Praise and thank Him for leading and directing our parents.

Phee Paradise

INTRODUCTION

How It All Began

John and Esther Shackelford met at San Francisco
Theological Seminary in 1942, where they were both preparing to
serve God on the mission field. John first noticed a beautiful
female student when he went to the library in the evenings to
check out books. Their meeting was no coincidence for Esther
was the librarian. She sat at the library desk and it was necessary
for John to converse with her in order to check out the books he
wanted to take to his room. Naturally, she needed a gallant young
student to walk her to the dorm at the bottom of the hill because it
was quite dark at ten at night. It was no surprise that soon they
stopped at a vacant bench along the path to the dorm for their
first kiss.

Esther was born in Paotingfu, China, where her parents were missionaries of the Presbyterian Board of Foreign Missions. She lived in China until she finished high school, when her parents felt she was mature enough to go to the States on her own. There she lived with an aunt and attended Santa Monica Junior College. When her parents came home on furlough she moved in with them and enrolled at Occidental College. After graduating in the summer of 1942, she worked at the conference center of the Presbyterian Church at Lake Tahoe where one evening she responded to God's call at the campfire and dedicated her life to service as a missionary. When Esther was challenged by an ardent evangelist who asked her if she was born again, she replied, "I have always believed in God and was taught as a child to give my life to Him. I knew that the Bible was God's Word and believed what it said about my salvation."

John was the son of a farmer in Garden Grove, California. His new life in Christ began on August 23, 1938 when he accepted Christ as his Savior while attending Santa Barbara State College. While searching for a personal relationship with God, he was given a little booklet titled, *The Reason Why*, by Robert Laidlaw. As he studied the little booklet he realized that he was not a Christian and when the booklet suggested that he could move into a relationship with the Omnipotent, Omniscient God by simply desiring it and asking Him to come into his life, he said yes to Him. After graduation, he went on to seminary where he served as student pastor at a church in Weed.

Esther and John graduated in 1943, now engaged to be married. Esther earned a master's degree in Christian education and John, with a master's in theology, was ordained by the Santa Barbara Presbytery. The wedding took place in the fall of that year at the Highland Park Presbyterian Church and was a marvelous event for them and their families. They were both accepted by the Presbyterian Board of Foreign Missions and, in 1945, were assigned to the mission field in Colombia, South America.

This book contains stories about the life of Esther and John Shackelford, but they are really stories of God reaching out to people to bless them, draw them into His Kingdom and teach them to walk with Him. These stories are much more than events that happened to two people; they tell how God is at work touching the lives of many people. They are the stories of God doing His work through events and circumstances in the Shackelford's lives. They all testify of His marvelous grace.

John's Call To Serve God

At my alma mater Santa Barbara State College, now the University of California at Santa Barbara, everyone was very proud of the insignia, a gaucho of Argentina. We were able to buy gaucho decals of different sizes which we placed on the windshields of our cars, notebooks and jackets to display our loyalty and pride for the football team and other events of the college. It was a major part of the art work in our yearbook. My favorite figure of the gaucho was about three inches tall and it was proudly displayed on everything that related to our school activities, events and sports. One of the decals of the gaucho was imprinted on the school notebook, which gave me an idea.

At the time my major was landscape architecture. This was a vocation that included courses in art and drawing, both line drawings as well as landscape design. One day a spirited conversation with another student moved me to carve a gaucho out of a bar of laundry soap and then mold it into lead so I could fasten it on the dash of my 1930 model A Ford. The piece of laundry soap was soft and I easily formed into my own gaucho by pasting the three inch tall decal figure onto the bar of soap and then carving all around it. I copied the proportions of the soap figure from the decal and this helped to keep it fairly authentic. It was a rather handsome figure and turned out to be very popular. Even though I had little experience in art this way, it was easy to keep the proper dimensions of the human figure.

It didn't take long to realize that a soap figure was not very durable in the rainy weather or when exposed to heat, which prompted me to make a sand mold and form a lead figure. In the high school shop we had been taught a very simple procedure for making cast figures by pouring melted lead into soft damp sand. This consisted of placing the object one wanted to copy into a two sided box and packing moist soft sand all around it. When the two sides were separated the soap figure was removed and the moist sand formed the shape of the object. One then poured melted lead into the space where the soap figure had been. In this case it was a gaucho. The lead copy had to be smoothed with sandpaper and then painted, but looked very much like the original. After adding a rope lasso and quirt, the gaucho was ready to display.

I couldn't wait to get home for the weekend to search the barn on our ranch to find some lead to make my first model. The search soon supplied a lot of lead weights that had been part of Dad's old fishing equipment. He had discarded them for new and better fishing weights and he quickly gave permission to melt the old lead sinkers and use them for the gaucho project. There was an iron ladle in the barn that had been used in melting light metals to repair farm equipment and pour bearings for the wagon wheels. It was just what was needed to melt the lead to pour into the sand mold.

Mother had always encouraged us in our little projects and let me use the burner on the gas stove in the kitchen to melt the lead. The ladle was about five inches in diameter and had a long handle so that one could hold it without burning his fingers. After heating the lead to the melting point I then rushed out to the moist sand mold conveniently placed just at the foot of the kitchen steps. It was easy to pour the mold full of the molten lead and it worked beautifully. As soon as the lead cooled I scraped away the sand to see the first lead figure that, to my eyes, was beautiful. The little figure did require a lot of sanding and filing to polish and finish it enough to resemble the original. After painting I fastened it to the dash of my Model A Ford and became the envy of any student who took notice. It took paint well and, needless to say, I was very proud of it.

Soon many students wanted a gaucho figure of their own. In fact, it was loved so much that it was ripped off the dash while I was in class and disappeared. That left a big hole in the dash and I was forced to make another to replace it. I quickly began to get requests from other students to make one for them — especially the girls. It never occurred to me to charge for them and I was still unaware this could become a home business. The figure had a nice metal base about two inches square and the weight of the lead made the gauchos into popular paperweights. I even made a set of bookends for one of the girls I was dating. By cutting a letter S for Santa Barbara out of one-inch plywood to make the back and another piece for the base, it made a very nice bookend.

By then I began to wise up. It was time to make some money from the project. During the depression, the only way to go to college was to do part-time work. We all had to work our way through school. I had worked as a gardener, dishwasher, and even usher in the Granada Theater to have money to pay my share of the rent. One especially unpleasant job I had was working by the hour for a couple of spinsters who had cats. My job was to take a pail of warm water with a heavy smell of ammonia and scrub the floors to get rid of the cat smell. It didn't take long to decide it was time for a more pleasant and lucrative job, so I welcomed the idea of making gaucho figures. My thoughts were that it would be a wonderful way to earn good money doing something I enjoyed. I was sure there was a ready market because of the demand from my friends. Consulting with others, we could see it had real merit. As we attended intercollegiate sporting events, and discussed the possibility, I realized that the other colleges had mascots too, and just maybe the business would grow into something big enough to sell at colleges and universities all over

Southern California. There was UCLA with its Bruin, Occidental with its Tiger and so on. At that point a friend told me that the figures really needed to be more professional, be carved by an artist and use cheaper material than lead if I was to make any money. So I began looking into buying an iron mold. With the original carved by an artist, it could become very professional. That way hundreds of gauchos could be manufactured cheaply instead of doing them one at a time in a sand mold. It would take less time and not require all of the filing and sanding and finish work. I began to seriously consider going into business for myself.

That is when God spoke to me. I had gone home for the weekend and was busy making several gaucho figures for my friends, when something incredible happened. As I knelt over one of the figures to pour the lead into the mold, I heard a distinct voice say to me, "This is the last one you are to make; don't pursue this project any further." It was very clear that God was speaking to me. It was He who said very clearly, "That's enough! I don't want you getting involved in something that will take so much of your time that you will not have time for Me."

That was the last gaucho I ever made. I didn't even keep one for myself. But last year my brother was cleaning out his garage and found one I had given him at the very beginning and he gave it back to me.

Now I look back on the wonderful life and ministry the Lord

gave to Esther and me, and realize how that project could have become so time consuming and lucrative that I would never have had time for the ministry. Possibly I would never have gone to seminary. That is where I met Esther and was trained to become a missionary. As I look back, I realize that in so many ways God's hand was leading us step by step and day by day.

That was the end of creating a major enterprise making gaucho statues but the beginning of a new life dedicated to honoring and serving the Lord. I later realized that it was just another example of: Jesus dosen't want your money but your life.

MISSION WORK

First Missionary Assignment
Sinú Valley, Colombia, 1946

In 1946, after nine months of language school in Medellín, Colombia, South America, we were assigned the supervision of the Presbyterian Churches in the Sinú Valley. This valley, which is formed by the river of the same name, is in the northwest area of Colombia near the Panamanian border. The previous missionary family assigned there had to resign and go home because of ill health. Later we discovered that there was a reason for that. Their infirmities came from living in that most difficult climate. Colombia is near the equator and the area is at sea level so it is tropical and very hot. It is inland and lacks costal breezes. Cereté is a very small town but we were assigned to live there because it had a missionary residence. The five room house with a bath was constructed with a tin roof and a wide open corridor that was the only way to get from room to room. The town has no doctor and is so demanding on your health that the term of service was only three years. Normally the Mission Board requires that each family serve at least five or more years each term before a furlough. There was a lot of serious discussion at the mission meeting as to whether we should even be assigned to the area since we were just out of language school and new to the mission field. After much discussion the missionaries finally agreed we should be assigned Cereté because, *"Esther had grown up on the mission field and was experienced enough to know how to handle tough assignments."* Furthermore, a missionary nurse, now learning Spanish at the language school, had been assigned to join us a year later.

After the mission decided on our assignment, Esther and I asked to live in Barranquilla temporarily until Peggy was born. The missionaries there had rented a large home to serve as a residence and a youth center and there was an empty room that we could occupy. Three missionary families lived there so that our combined rent allowance would pay the landlord. They had decided that this was the only way to afford a youth center for the several churches in Barranquilla. After getting settled in, Dick Shaul, our assigned senior missionary, informed me that we were leaving the following week to make an introductory visit to the Sinú Valley.

Dick informed me that we would take the army surplus Jeep that belonged to the mission. The vehicle had just been purchased from the army surplus pool in Panama and was ideal for this type of work. It truly would be necessary inasmuch as the roads actually reverted to jungle during the six month's wet season; for in the tropics the rain, mud, and ardent growth soon takes over and all trails are obliterated. During the rainy season, no vehicle was able to travel over those jungle roads. The wet season was about to begin and travel would soon be limited to the slow river boat or horseback. All these were reasons why Dick felt we should leave at once even though the baby was soon due.

Our first stop was the city of Cartagena, about two hours away. We stopped there long enough to visit the native pastor and his wife and to talk about the Sinú churches and what we could expect. Then we drove for another two hours under the hot sun to the little town of Sincelejo where the Latin American Mission had a clinic and a mission station with several missionaries in residence. That was a good place to stop because they offered us cool lemonade made with boiled water *and ice.* We had been warned by the mission nurse never to drink the water on the trip or we would come down with dysentery. Once, when I was not careful, that threat became real and I was disgraced because to get sick meant that one had disregarded the mission's medical advice. In fact most of our lives on the mission field we had to boil all the water that we drank and even the water we used in cooking. Vegetables could not be eaten raw and fruit had to be soaked with chlorine which took away much of the taste and turned it black. The only exception was what could be peeled, such as bananas and mangos if one was careful not to touch the fruit as you peeled it. A cork screw was twisted into a mango to serve as a holder so you could keep it clean. Such foods as strawberries were *never eaten!*

After another long drive on the dusty dirt road, we arrived at Cereté where we were greeted by the faithful elder, Señor

Thelwell and his wife. They were prominent citizens of the town and kept the church alive. They were from Jamaica, well educated, and very anxious that the town have a prominent Protestant church. On arrival, we were greeted warmly and they expressed great joy seeing the new missionary for they had a project already waiting for me. Señor Thelwell and his wife invited us in and offered us a nice warm shower, a very good dinner and interesting conversation. Their comfortable beds were on the side of the house where there were cool coco palm trees. Their home proved to be a great oasis on many occasions. The whole dusty trip was almost worth such a super reception. Señor Thelwell pointed out the house across the river where Esther and I were to live and where the project was waiting for me. They had long waited for the Mission to raise the funds to build a church. Finally, the funds had been approved but there was no one to direct the construction. An old brick house and the missionary home sat on the mission property. The renovated brick house was small but served as a temporary church and day school. The new church would be built between the two buildings.

The Thelwells spent most of the dinner hour telling us how glad they were to finally have a missionary on the spot. Of course, they wanted to know where my wife was and showed real disappointment when told that we were expecting a baby and Esther had to stay in Barranquilla, where there was a nice clinic and a doctor. Esther would care for Peggy there until she was old enough to travel. Señor Thelwell was willing to wait for Esther since I was available to begin the construction right away. We quickly agreed on a compromise. I would travel back and forth from Cereté to Barranquilla and thus be able to supervise the construction of the new church. They were quite satisfied with this arrangement. Señor and Señora Thelwell offered to give me board and room for the days I would be in town. He offered to show Dick and me around the next day, but that evening we were to go to the old brick building that served as a church for a special meeting. The congregation was waiting to take a good look at the new missionary.

My part time residence was technically a very wise decision, for it meant that the members of the church, especially the elders, would have to be deeply involved in erecting *their* new building. That was a great lesson for me in missiology, for it proved that if a person is not involved in a program, such as building a new church, he is only partially interested and really does not have any sense of ownership. The building was paid for by the mission and they would not really feel responsible for it until they had to take part in the construction and make some of the decisions about its looks and type of construction.

After some lengthy discussion, it was decided that a cement block building would be best for that hot climate. Cinder block construction would be cooler on hot nights when there was no breeze and the church was full of people. The next step was to find where cement blocks were made and sold. I guess we were way ahead of our time, for there was no such thing as a cement block factory in that whole valley. The only way to build with cinder blocks was to make our own molds and pour the cement ourselves. I showed the elders how to make several molds to create the cement blocks and they offered to find and supervise the workers who were to mix the cement and pour the blocks during the days I would be away.

I explained that this would take a lot of blocks and the work must go on even if I were not there. This appealed to them for now they wanted to be a part of the construction and Señor Thelwell actually helped me pour the first block during a special church service of groundbreaking. They soon learned to make a few blocks and were excited to be building their own church. By the time Dick and I left to visit the churches upriver they were hard at work.

We drove the faithful jeep another five hours up country to visit about three or four villages where the mission had established churches. Some were run by elders and two had their own pastors. The mission subsidized these pastors because there was no way these tiny congregations could support them. So the mission either helped them financially or the pastor had to farm small areas of his own, to keep his family in food. The homes were simple. There was no big "cost of living" problem because they all raised corn and rice in their back yards.

Dick and I slept in our hammocks that we strung up in the corridor of a home. After three or four days of preaching and checking on the work, using the town of Nazarét as our headquarters, we were ready to start for home. Nazarét was a large village, and my next project was to build a home and clinic for the two mission nurses who were to be assigned to assist the people in that whole area. Dick Baird, a former missionary, had purchased a large tract of land with mission money to establish this village for Christians who had been dispossessed of their land and driven out by those who hated Protestants.

By the time we were ready to start home, Dick had come down with a very high fever and chills. That was my first experience with malaria, and it scared me because we had no medicine or medical help. At his command, I drove as fast as I could to Sincelejo where the missionary nurses who had earlier given us the lemonade took him in. They gave him quinine and the next day got him on the DC3 flight which landed on their local dirt strip once a day, and had him flown back home to Barranquilla. At home, the doctor was able to slowly bring him back to health.

When I got as far as Cereté I stopped to see how the cement blocks were going. Upon arrival I discovered they had all worked hard and poured the cement foundation for the church. I stayed through Sunday so the members of the church could have a service to lay the first block. There was a pastor in Cereté, and the elders and members came outside after worship and we laid the cornerstone (block) for the new church in the customary fashion.

The next day I was able to head for home over the same dirt and dusty road. I drove those many miles alone through rivers and jungle, but it was a happy time because I was headed home to Esther. Upon arrival, I was quickly informed that Peggy was born while I was away. But I was forgiven by all because there was no way to phone me or to communicate with me until I drove in the driveway. I was a new daddy, they told me, as Esther and Peggy smiled up at me from the hospital bed!

Men's Prayer Group
Quetzaltenango, Guatemala, 1951

In 1882, the Dictator Justo Rufino Barrios invited a
Presbyterian missionary to Guatemala. Soon after the work in
Guatemala City was started, the Presbyterian Church in
Quetzaltenango was established. Quetzaltenango is the second
largest city in Guatemala and many of the residents are owners of
large coffee *fincas* on the skirts of the volcano between this 8,000
foot city and the Pacific Coast. The city is also in the center of
the Mayan Quiché peoples of the country. It is a cultured city,
having a large old fashioned opera house and a university. The
mission was able to purchase property on the plaza, next to the
opera house, and they built a beautiful stone church which is
attended by both leaders of the educated Hispanics and the
Mayan population.

These educated leaders responded very quickly to our
suggestion that they should form a morning fellowship and
prayer group during the week. Their decision was to meet at 6:00
a.m. two days a week for prayer. It was a great pleasure to be part
of that group, though it meant getting up in that cold climate
when often there was still ice on the ground. They did not heat
their homes and praying on your knees on the cement floors was
a real challenge. Once a month they took turns inviting the group

to their homes for breakfast and the pastor or missionary would bring a short devotional. With a hymn or two and black beans and tortillas, the breakfasts became a legend. Part of the success of the church was clearly because of this active and enthusiastic band of prayer partners. After the prayer time they disbanded to go to work. Through these meetings there sprung up a new fellowship and loyalty both to each other and to the church. Being in their homes had given us friendships and a loyalty to Christ that we hardly believed possible. We can truly say there are no barriers of culture or race to separate us because of our fellowship in the Lord. Some think that foreigners and even sometimes missionaries were unwelcome in the Latin culture, but we had never had more real friends nor closer companionship than we found among these men whom we came to love dearly.

As the vacation time came near and our schedule of summer conferences was taking shape, these men made this a major subject of their prayers. They often prayed for certain youth they wanted to go to camp and that God would work major changes in their lives. We had plans for the retreats in the towns of El Rancho, Lake Amatitlán, and Lake Atitlán. The youth from Quetzaltenango would go to Lake Atitlán. Those who lived in the arid, desert area on the railroad from Guatemala City to the Caribbean Coast would be able to travel to El Rancho on the narrow gauge railroad built by the United Fruit Company and the folks from Guatemala City would be able to get to Lake

Amatitlán by bus which is only 30 kilometers from the many Presbyterian churches in the capital city. Facilities were very primitive but the response was enthusiastic and positive.

It was for these camps the men in Quetzaltenango prayed and there is no doubt that the very presence of the Lord and the very positive response to spiritual things came about because of their asking the Lord to make it happen. In each conference, the Lord gave great victory in the lives of the campers and grace to live in a way that many of them had never dreamed possible. There is no doubt that God met us there and many youth who accepted Christ discovered the Christian life is possible and desirable. The prayers and influence of the men in this prayer group gave all of us a new perspective about prayer and the work of God in the church.

An Unexpected Knock
on the Door
Quetzaltenango, Guatemala, 1952

It was late morning. I was at my desk in the study and Esther
was in the kitchen. Suddenly there was a very hard knock on the
door. We were living at the old mission house next door to the
church that had been built in the early 1900s by one of the first
Presbyterian missionaries to Guatemala. The house had two huge
doors built of heavy wood big enough to drive a carriage through.
The door on the right had an old Spanish-style knocker about six
inches long. It was made of two parts, a huge lion head on a
hinge that was used for knocking on a base. The visitor knew
how to use it and we could hear the knock throughout the whole
house.

I opened the door to see two Mayan Quiché Indians. Before I
could ask them who they were or what I could do for them, they
burst out, "Queremos aceptar a Jesucristo." Their Spanish was
limited and I was ignorant of their Mayan language but I
understood that they said. "We want to accept Jesus Christ." I
was taken aback, for seldom does anyone take that kind of
initiative anywhere — much less in the Mayan culture. After a
moment, when I got my senses back, I invited them to come into
the living room. Indians were seldom welcome in Spanish homes;

many of them were from the country, and lived in very humble huts. Their culture and position in society had taught them to stand to talk or maybe sit on the corridor bench along an outside wall, yet they gingerly accepted my invitation and timidly walked through the patio and covered walkway, with its rough stepping stones, into the house.

They sat on the front of their chairs as though uncomfortable, but they were determined. They spoke out again and said, "Hemos venido para aceptar a Cristo."

"We have come to accept Christ," were their words.

How do you start explaining the gospel when minds are already made up? I had been taught the normal approach. We try to help others understand the existence of God before inviting them to accept Christ. First we ask one if he believes in God. Then we tell him about the Bible and its condemnation of sin. From there we quote several scripture verses that explain how Jesus came to die for our sins. But this time I had to say a silent prayer and try to find the words I needed to help them. They sat there waiting. I just felt led to quote several verses that spoke of Jesus' death on the cross to save us from our sins, and asked them if they understood.

"Yes, that is what we want!" they replied emphatically. I spoke to them individually and asked each point blank, "Do you invite Jesus Christ into your heart and life?" Each one emphatically replied, "Yes!" So I led them in prayer, asking them to repeat after me the words, "Dear Jesus Christ, I am sorry for my sins and I invite You to come into my life as Savior and Lord. I ask You for forgiveness and thank You for dying on the cross to give me a new life in You. Please come into my life and give me salvation."

Each one prayed that prayer after me and I then read several verses from the Bible that confirmed that Jesus could and did give them a new life in Christ. After a few minutes of silence, one of them burst out, "I think we have made a mistake."

That so took me by surprise that I just sat in silence. Then he said, "Our wives are outside in the street. They need to come in and accept Christ also."

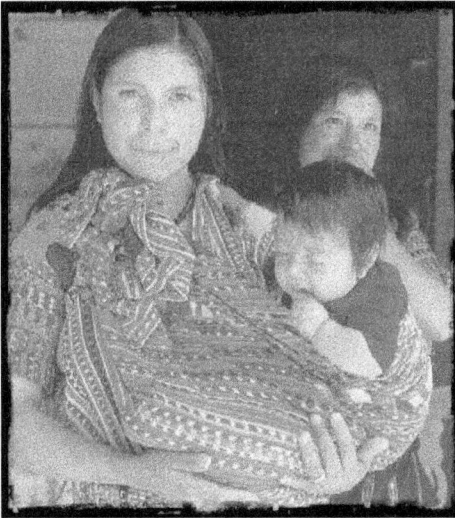

I had been afraid they might mean that they wanted to recant and was rather relieved when I realized what they were saying. Timidly, one of them said, "Can we bring them into your house and let them also accept Christ?"

"Of course," I replied, but realized I was in trouble, for the women could not speak any Spanish and I didn't know more than *good morning* and *how are you* in their language. By then Esther had come into the room to say hello to the visitors and be gracious to them. As she saw the women coming in, she realized the dilemma I was in.

"Why don't I ask Edelmira, our maid, to talk to them," she said. "She is a Mayan Christian, and knows how to help them make a decision for Christ."

Edelmira had studied at the Mission Quiché Bible Institute and had experience speaking of Christ with her own people. As a student, she had even gone to some of the Indian villages to take part in their evangelistic meetings. She came in and greeted them in their own language, then sat down with them to respond to their questions. They were so excited to find someone who could understand. Soon I saw them all nodding and showing a very positive, enthusiastic response.

As they got up to leave, God gave me the great idea of giving them some phonograph records in the Quiché language. Joy Ridderhoff of Los Angeles had visited the country to gather around her some Indian pastors. They had recorded several sermons, some singing, and the reading of several key Scripture verses on the old 78 records, with three minutes of speaking on each side, and I had several sets. In order to listen to them, she had also given us a simple windup phonograph that could play the records without electricity. It was not the modern audio wonder of today, but they could hear the gospel in their own language and were thrilled when I played one of the records for them. Even before I could offer it to them, one of them asked me if they could buy it and take it back to their village so their neighbors could hear them too. I told them that it was a gift from a Christian sister from the United States and I wanted to give it to them. But they insisted that they would not impose on me and that they must pay for it. They drew some bills from their pockets and then walked away with a super smile on their faces, carrying in their arms the small phonograph and records as though their lives depended on not breaking them.

But it didn't end there. A few days later, they were back asking if they could buy some more records. They told me that they had played them over and over for the whole village and the records were all worn out. All they could hear now was a scratch and it was impossible to understand them anymore. I did have a small supply, and we quickly wrapped some more for them to take home.

I asked where they were from, thinking that there must be a way to follow up on this great opportunity and get another missionary involved. Stan Wick, the Director of the Quiché Bible Institute, could take students to visit and maybe find some of the neighbors who would like to know Christ too. Stan looked up the village on the map and discovered it was in the area of the Primitive Methodist Mission. Since we had a good rapport with all the other missionaries, we cooperated closely and respected any existing work they might have in progress. There were so many villages without the gospel that there was no need to do any "sheep stealing." Loren and Helen Anderson from the Methodist Mission were working hand in hand with our Presbyterian Mission at the Quiché Bible Institute, so we went over to talk to Loren about the exciting time I had with these people and ask him if the Methodists would be able to visit them and follow up what had been started in that village.

He seemed very surprised and burst out, "That village will have nothing to do with the gospel! We visited them several times and they always drove us away. We almost gave up on them and resorted only to prayer. This is God's answer to our prayers. We tried several times to hold services there."

In the next few days, he gathered some of the students and they visited the village of the new converts. They came back ecstatic; not only were they given a warm welcome, they discovered that almost all the people of the village were gathering regularly to sing the songs they had learned from the records, were listening to the sermons, and had memorized all the Scripture verses and even the prayers. The church was already established. All Loren had to do was introduce himself. I think God has a great sense of humor to use a Presbyterian Missionary to start a Methodist Church.

Bob's First Communion in Guatemala

Dr. Robert Thorp, 1947

The Presbyterian churches in Guatemala did not all have pastors so most of the missionaries were called to supply several churches, which meant preaching about once a month in each, moderating the session and serving communion once a quarter. Consequently, each ordained missionary was called upon quarterly to go to one or more churches. Bob Thorp was fresh out of seminary and had just arrived in Guatemala. He was asked by veteran missionary, Harry Peters, to help him serve communion in a small rural town.

Bob relates that he had been properly ordained in his home church in the United States and part of his seminary training was how to lead the very formal Holy Communion Worship Service as it should be done in a denomination that prided itself in doing things properly and in order. The communion service was a sacrament of the church and was to be a very sacred time. Dr. White, the seminary professor, was very careful to instill in his students just how they should dress, the proper tone of voice, and how the table and communion elements should be placed on the table. It was imperative that the linen cloth and napkins should be freshly laundered and properly ironed and the communion cups were to be filled without letting even one drop stain the linens. The cups were carefully placed in the silver tray with a compartment for each cup and the wine was already poured into the silver chalice. The deacons were to carefully prepare all before the service. Of course, the service was planned in detail, the table moved to its proper place before the pulpit, and the elements carefully positioned long before anyone would enter the sanctuary.

The training also included using just the right words and the timing was carefully coordinated so that each part of the service would be dependent on the other. The elders, properly dressed in black suits, were to be trained to march forward in a stately fashion and to stand on the very spot the pastor had marked on the carpet with a little chalk mark. Each one was instructed just which row and in what order they were to serve. If any children were present they were not to partake until they had been baptized. The training of the elders took place at a special meeting held previous to the Sunday worship service.

Bob had never had the opportunity to serve communion to a church in the United States and so was anxious that his first communion in Guatemala would be beautiful and proper, just as the professor had taught him in seminary. Harry Peters and Bob left for a rural church in El Rancho where Harry would preach and together they would serve communion.

Being a rural church in the desert area of the Motagua

Valley, the evening was hot and sweaty. The *campesinos* were farmers and for the most part their bathing facility was the river after the day's work. The wives and children often bathed as they did the family wash on the stones at the bank of the river. By the time they got to church in the evening, the tin roof building was hot and steamy and not a single elder owned a tie or a coat. It simply was not needed in these rural areas of the tropics.

The service was traditional and consisted of a message, singing, and prayer. These rural folks sang well and enthusiastically. The children were quiet and attentive and sitting in the front row as usual. Bob did his part well, leading in prayer, and directing the singing. But there was no sign of the communion table as he had been taught in seminary, no linens nor grape juice in a silver chalice.

Bob was concerned and turned to whisper to Harry, during the last hymn before serving the communion, to ask, "Where are the elements?"

Harry replied, "Don't worry, Bob, they will take care of it."

As they got to the last verse of the communion hymn there was still no sign of movement by the deacons and this concerned Bob. Again he asked, "When do they bring in the communion elements?"

"Don't worry," whispered Harry, seemingly not at all concerned.

Sure enough, just as the music ended, in came one of the

deacons carrying an unpainted kitchen table, inverted over his head so the legs would not hit anyone in the pews. He marched down the center aisle and placed the table at the front of the sanctuary. The obviously well used table, darkened with many washings of lye, was set down right in front of the pulpit. The deacon then turned and quickly walked out, having performed his part of the communion worship service. Within minutes, a deaconess walked down the aisle carrying a folded kitchen oilcloth which she smoothed out over the table, and she then walked down the aisle to her seat. Now the time had come for the pastors to come down from the platform and Harry motioned to Bob to pick up his chair. Together they walked down the platform steps, placed their chairs behind the table and seated themselves. But the kitchen table, now converted into a sacred communion table, still lacked the bread and the grape juice.

Harry began the communion service with a prayer and Bob covertly looked around to try to find out how the grape juice and bread would appear. As soon as the prayer was over, the deaconess appeared at the door, walked down the aisle with a washbasin full of communion cups that rattled loudly because they struck each other on the rounded bottom of the pan. Another trip brought a tin plate from the kitchen with a couple of tortillas on it. These were placed on the table and the woman went over and sat down. Bob was still concerned because there was no grape juice, but before he could question Harry, an elder appeared with a bottle of warm grape soda pop that he had purchased in the little cantina across the street. This he ceremoniously placed on the table. It obviously was nice and warm and shaken up on the trip.

As the time neared to bless the elements, Bob reached over slyly and tried to flip the cap off the carbonated drink. To his consternation it was sealed tight. He knew he did not have a bottle opener hidden in his trouser pockets and quietly turned to Harry to ask if he had one. But Harry didn't come equipped either.

"What will I do?" whispered Bob, for they were about to serve the bread. About then the congregation was getting more interested in Bob's dilemma than in the decor of the service, and an elder quickly jumped up, took the room temperature bottle, and tried to pry the top off by hooking it on a nail that stuck out from the wooden plank steps of the platform. But it was useless, nothing was about to loosen the bottle cap.

All inspiration and quiet was gone by then, and the whole congregation was concentrating on how the elder was to get that bottle open. After a couple of tries, one of the young boys near the front jumped up and took a nail out of his pocket, and in front of everyone, pried at the top till it came loose. Now Bob had to pour out that hot grape soda pop into the rattling cups. What a delightful job it turned out to be.

Later Bob said to us, "Have you ever tried to pour hot carbonated grape drink that has been well shaken up?" It was a good thing the cups were in the dishpan!

But there were not enough cups to go around, and again Bob whispered to Harry, "What do I do now?"

The experienced deaconess supplied the answer as she gathered the used glasses, and dumped them into a waiting pail of cold water sitting on the floor by the communion table. She then reached in and swished the water around and brought out the wet cups and returned them to the waiting tray. It was easy to see that Bob was to refill them and give them to an elder who was waiting until he could serve the rest of the waiting congregation.

Later, as Bob told us about this unique communion service, he was sure that Dr. White, of the seminary, must have turned over in his grave. However, we were all convinced that these simple *campesinos* of Guatemala were as blessed, or even more so, than we who have been served with all our pomp and ceremony. God has a way of reaching out to these people in ways that we cannot even imagine.

The Coat on the Wall
Tiquizate, Guatemala, 1952

The Presbyterian Church in the tropical town of Tiquizate, Guatemala, is a barnlike structure of wood construction with a sizzling tin roof. Even late at night it is never cool in the church; since there is no air-conditioning or even small fans in Tiquizate it is hot even into the evening. The walls are of clapboard construction with no interior finish or paint, just the rough boards twelve inches wide cut on a primitive saw mill. Windows are cut out of the wall to make a simple opening and the removed boards are nailed into hinged shutters with hinges added so they can be closed when the church is not in use or when it rains. The windows are opened every time there is a service to catch any small breeze. The church was built with mission funds for the laborers of the banana groves of the United Fruit Company plantation. The workers had migrated to this company town, which is located on the west coast of Guatemala.

On a visit to the church, my eye was drawn to the heavy wool coat hanging on a 20-penny nail driven into the wall just behind the pulpit. It was completely out of place in the chancel which is the strategic point of worship. The platform took up the whole width of the building at one end of the 300 member church, but it was bare of religious symbols and only the wool coat hung there. It obviously was the kind worn in the highlands where it is quite cold, but here the men in Tiquizate didn't even own a white cotton coat much less a black wool one. For obvious reasons heavy wool coats are never worn in the tropics.

The congregation comes in freshly laundered and ironed work clothes, all spruced up for their Sunday best. Most of the men work in the banana fields, which are hot and dirty. The juice of the banana stalks badly stains their clothing and they are always sweaty, but they come to church freshly laundered. The women have to work hard to keep up their simple homes and some of them take in laundry to help their meager income. Furthermore, it takes lots of extra work to keep the children clean in a town of sandy, dusty streets, and a very hot sun.

It was the custom to have various members of the congregation take part in announcing the hymns, leading in prayer and the reading of Scripture. The leader always invited the congregation to stand when the Scriptures were read. He explained to me that in respect for the Word of God they always stand when it is read. Standing for the singing of the hymns seemed to be at the discretion of the pastor. The music was only accompanied by a small portable pump organ, but it was loud and everyone was enthusiastic. Because the church was full, the children, of which there were many, sat on the cement floor right in front of the pulpit, but they were quiet and well behaved. Of course, I was asked to sit on the platform with the pastor and I only had on my white shirt with short sleeves and a tie. I felt a bit out of place when I saw that the pastor had on a nice white cotton coat. I had not expected his dressing up in that climate.

Then I discovered why the coat was on the nail behind the pulpit. As each person came to the pulpit to lead in prayer, read Scripture or just make an announcement, he went to the coat, took it off the nail and put it on before moving into the sacred spot behind the pulpit. It was almost a symbol and it seems that there was an unwritten rule of that Presbytery, where most of its churches are located in the cool highlands: that no one was to enter that special spot behind the pulpit without wearing a coat. A tie was never worn, nor was a clean shirt important, but you never occupied that spot without a coat. Since the leaders of the church didn't own coats in that tropical coastal plain, the elders had been careful to provide one for those who were to stand before the congregation. A black wool coat if you please!

Since I was to preach that night, I stood behind the pulpit in shirt sleeves and a tie but in ignorance read Scripture and prayed, and even preached, without a coat. It wasn't until later that I was advised that I should have brought my coat with me, or used the hot, sweaty black wool coat even though it didn't fit and the sleeves were too short. I had thought the coat was out of place in the chancel and not worshipful at all, but to the people of Tiquizate it was a symbol of respectful worship.

The Evangelist Fails to Show
Coatepeque, Guatemala, 1952

Don Ramón Cabrera was a Cuban evangelist invited to Guatemala to have a series of evangelistic meetings in many of our Presbyterian churches. We were living in Quetzaltenango at the time; Esther and I were assigned to visit churches in the area and help them establish Christian Endeavor societies and youth programs.

My schedule was flexible and so I was assigned to be don Ramón's chauffeur and promote these evangelistic meetings in the Spanish speaking churches of Sija, Sibilia, Coatepeque, Tiquizate, and several other smaller towns on the Pacific Coast. Our first meeting was to be in the rather large town of Coatepeque at the bottom of the *cordillera* on the Pacific coastal plain. The mission had established a large church there but it was hard to find a good pastor and they often asked the missionary to moderate the session meetings and preach. There was a deep concern that these evangelistic meetings be a great success and bring in new church members. Don Ramón was a very capable evangelist but we still felt the burden of prayer so I asked don Oscar Barrientos, the pastor of Bethel Church in Quetzaltenango, to join me each morning for a couple of weeks in the sanctuary to pray specifically for these evangelistic meetings. Don Oscar was no stranger to prayer. He had spent his youth as a member of a family of revolutionaries and had been converted through the prayer of a missionary family in Chiquimula so he knew that prayer was God's way of truly making changes in people's lives.

We got together each morning about 9:00 and knelt by the front pew of the church to pray that God would be gracious and bring many into His Kingdom. Quetzaltenango is cold and the church had no heating. We prayed in overcoats but we felt moved to go there and pray anyway. I still remember how cold it was, and how my knees almost gave out, but don Oscar was deeply concerned about God's working in the lives of the people on the coast and never seemed to mind.

The day came for the first meeting and I drove down to Coatepeque in the morning to meet with the session for prayer. Then we drove through town announcing the meetings with the public address system fastened to the roof of the car. The mission had inherited this bulky equipment from the army after World War II. Then we placed the loud speakers in the church tower so the large crowd outside of the church could hear also. One of the elders commented that he hoped that many in the community would also hear so we placed the speakers in the bell tower. He insisted that it be turned up to full volume. This was an exciting event for the whole town as there was no theater in town except on Saturday night when movies were shown in a makeshift arena. TV had not been introduced yet and so this was big entertainment for everyone.

At about 6:00 p.m., the hour that the old steam train was to arrive, we rushed off to the railroad station. Don Ramón was to arrive on that train from the churches on the Atlantic side of the country. The train arrived on time, and we went to look for the evangelist. After several minutes the train blew its whistle and pulled away for Las Palmas, which is near the Mexican border. But don Ramón was not on the train. **He didn't show up!** What a blow! The meetings had been announced and the whole town invited but we could not find the evangelist. We looked all around the station and checked to be sure he had not started off to town on foot along with the crowd, but he simply was not there. What were we to do? Flyers had been distributed, the church people were all enthusiastic about his coming, the elders were waiting at the church where their wives had prepared a nice welcoming dinner under the trees in the church patio. Everyone was excited about the big event coming to town, but our evangelist had disappeared into thin air!

I skipped dinner, and called the elders into the study to decide what to do. The small two room manse was also the Sunday school meeting room and the study. There was no other room where we could meet. We talked about the problem, how it would affect the church, and the attitude of the townspeople towards us and the gospel if we didn't do something to entertain the crowd. Some people in town had been antagonistic in the past because of a problem between the church and the cantina across the street. The church was strongly opposed to such a business on their doorstep, and had been active in getting it closed down.

The elders and I decided it best to pray first, and I reminded them of the long hours don Oscar and I had spent praying in Quetzaltenango to ask God to bless the meetings and give us many converts. Who would preach in this emergency, and how could we solve the problem of no evangelist? The elders had a ready answer. They simply said, "You are the missionary, you will have to preach." Well, I didn't have any sermon prepared, nor did I have any experience preaching as a professional evangelist, but they insisted. So with just a few minutes before the service was to start I got alone and looked for a few passages in my Bible that would be appropriate. I decided to use several verses about salvation such as John 3:16, Romans 3:3 and Romans 3:6 along with II Corinthians 5:17, which talks about becoming a new person in Christ.

We had a packed house; in fact, many folks were standing around outside looking in through the open door and windows of the church. Many had gathered around the door chatting, some smoking, others just interested, but all were waiting for the big event. After a couple of hymns and prayer, an elder greeted the crowd with a typical Latin welcome. He then shared the church's enthusiasm for the event and greeted the visitors on the outside and told them that don Ramón had not shown up, but that the *Norteamericano* would preach instead. I doubt that it made much difference to the people for it was a social event for the town and they were having a good time. Not many of the congregation were highly educated, although we did have a few dignitaries in the audience. We sang several more hymns, prayed, and read the Bible passages I had chosen.

I gave a simple introduction, and before I could say more, a little boy, seated about half way down the sanctuary, sitting on the right side with his father, held up his hand. The father pulled the hand down, and I went on, but the child lifted his hand again. Finally, he just stood up to get my attention. The father scolded him and tried to get him to sit down and be quiet. But by then I realized that the Holy Spirit was working in a special way, and I asked the boy what he wanted. Such a simple, remarkable statement, "*Quiero aceptar a Cristo* (I want to accept Christ) Isn't that what we came for?"

But I hadn't even finished my sermon! Don't preachers have an introduction and three points to make before they give the altar call? There was nothing to do but to stop preaching and talk to him in a personal way. I didn't leave the pulpit but we carried on our conversation in front of the congregation and I told him how to become a Christian.

He said, "Yes! that is what I want to do, that is why I came tonight!" I led him in a prayer of forgiveness for sin and of giving his life to God, and he repeated my simple prayer out loud, even repeating the mistakes I made in Spanish, and became a Christian right then and there.

After he sat down, I again felt the moving of the Holy Spirit, not to preach, but to give an invitation. I asked if there was anyone else who wanted to be a Christian. Mind you, I had not preached yet! Would you believe it! Between 15 and 20 people stood up, men women and children, and they all expressed the same desire to know God. The Lord had answered the intercession that don Oscar and I had prayed for in Bethel Church in Quetzaltenango. God didn't need a sermon at all for there was no need to preach. He had already done His work in their hearts in answer to our prayer.

The next day don Ramón arrived on the evening train ready to take over from me. We found that he had had a great response in the churches in El Rancho and the nearby villages and he had stayed on to preach to them for a few extra days. He also showed us how to have a good follow-up of the new converts in Coatepeque. We invited them to come the next day and he explained the meaning of becoming a new Christian and how to live for Christ every day. The elders were also blessed as they saw that conversions are the work of the Holy Spirit when the congregation turns to Him in prayer. They also learned how to take the responsibility to teach the new converts the way of God in their lives. They now saw how important it was for the elders to minister to the congregation. The other nights the pews filled as God continued to bring more people into His Kingdom. By the way, don Ramón is a much better evangelist than I and did a great job preaching a full sermon each of the following evenings. And with many converts.

Don Ramón Cabrera
Evangelistic Campaign
Tiquizate, Guatemala, 1952

Our campaign with don Ramón Cabrera was a winner from the beginning. The Presbyterian Church in Guatemala had given their official sanction to this campaign and was enthusiastic about his coming. Don Ramón taught me many things about sharing the love of Christ. Whenever we were invited to stay in a believer's home, he would teach the family to pray for each other and for the unbelievers in the community. As he led in the morning devotions, they learned to pray for the evangelistic campaigns.

He always based his prayer time on Scripture and they counted it a blessing to have us stay with them. As we took our leave from their home to move to another town, he would say to the hosts, "We don't have any way to reimburse you for the expenses you have had, but we can ask God to bless and prosper you." And then he would pray for the home, the head of the house and their work, and then commend them and their life in Christ to God.

In the United Fruit Company owned town of Tiquizate the church was filled a long time before the meetings were to begin. Television did not yet exist. There was a movie house in town, but it only showed movies on Saturday nights, so we were the big attraction all week. The church was so full that the elders brought all the children forward and sat them on the cement floor in front of the pulpit. It was hot and smelly and enthusiastic, but the children were very quiet and well behaved. Whenever a baby would cry, the preacher would interrupt his sermon and say to the mother, 'Please feed your baby," (meaning to breast feed) and the mother immediately complied.

Since the people were there way ahead of time, we organized a choir to sing until the preaching began. The choir had to sit on the big platform because all the pews were full. They had never studied music, and as director I had never had a lesson in leading a choir, but our singing was joyful and loud. In the history of the church there had never been a choir and most of the town had never heard of one so it was easy to perform. Furthermore, not all sang in tune, but the portable pump organ helped them stay on key. We simply sang familiar hymns so it was not necessary to read music. In fact their hymn books didn't even have the notes printed out, only the words. That made the book smaller and consequently cheaper. Everyone had to bring his own hymnal as the church did not provide any. It may have been my first experience as a choir director and their first as a choir, but God blessed them and incidentally made more space in the pews for the visitors. Somehow word got around that we had a choir and this no doubt attracted some of the non-church people of the pueblo. The windows only had shutters and no glass, and because of the heat they were all open on those hot tropical nights. The curious and those who could not get a seat gathered several deep at the windows and at the doors to watch and listen.

Our itinerary took us to preach in several churches along the Pacific coastal plain. Each church had been sent a telegram well ahead of time and they organized special prayer meetings for the evangelistic campaign which generated great interest. But, right in the middle of the month of meetings a revolution started. The morning of the second day of the fighting, we were preaching at the church in Cuyotenango. The minute the pastor got word, he rushed to our room to warn us. He was very frightened and did not want to hold any more public meetings. On the spot, he canceled the meeting for that night; we spent a lot of time in prayer on that one. The news came over the government radio station about 10:00 a.m. and so we had most of the day to decide what to do. The lack of enthusiasm on the part of the pastor was kind of a warning. Don Ramón was also very fearful, and told us that when he was preaching in Guayaquil, the West Coast port city of Ecuador, a big revolution started there. They were shot at several times as the church was right in the center of the fighting. He shared with us how the fighting got so close to the church that bullets and men with machetes came right into the sanctuary. I don't remember that he reported any church members being killed, but his story convinced us all that our preaching in Guatemala was over.

We packed up our suitcases and the public address system and by then it was time for lunch. After eating we drove the few miles to Mazatenango, the department head where there was a military base. I wanted to consult with the commander and find out just where the fighting was and how serious it was. The big question was, "Is there a curfew and are public meetings allowed?" Whenever there was fighting in the country, the Government declared that civil liberty was withheld and public gatherings of more than three or four people in public were prohibited. We were afraid what the police would think when they saw the PA system in the car. I think that was the first time I heard the famous phrase, "If you don't like the government, wait five minutes."

The commander had not prohibited public meetings yet but he was not anxious for us to have a large public meeting that night. He advised us to go home and do our preaching at another time. He was not antagonistic however. The evangelistic crusade had come to a standstill even though there had not been an

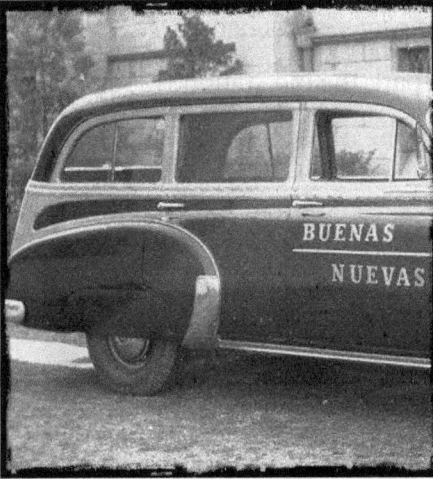

official prohibition of public meetings. So again, Don Ramón prayed ardently for us and for the people we were to preach to. We also had to send telegrams to the churches telling them that we felt led to cancel our meetings in their town.

Sending telegrams was the only reliable communication in those days because few people had telephones. But it was rapid and reliable. The charge was three cents a word and we always sent telegrams to advise family and friends of our activities.

We had been on the coastal plain in the tropics and the drive home to Quetzaltenango took us to an altitude of 8,000 ft. over dirt roads. Fearful that we might run into bands of rebels, we started home as soon as possible, not wanting to drive at night. It was still daylight when we arrived home safely to the old mission house where Esther and I lived and we had not been stopped or shot at on that seemingly endless three hour drive. We contacted the veteran missionary, don Pablo Burgess, who was my advisor and told him what had happened. He was disappointed and reprimanded us. He called us cowards, and told us of the many times he had been jailed and even had secretly kept some revolutionaries in the attic of his house during the dictatorship of General Cabrera. I guess his perspective was better than mine, but I still was glad to get home, park the old station wagon where it was safe in the garage, and eat one of Esther's nice warm meals.

A Different Kind of Synod Meeting
Retalhuleu, Guatemala, 1953

Adolfo Martinez was pastor of the large Retalhuleu
Presbyterian Church on the Pacific Coast and famous for being a
great barefoot evangelist. Adolfo and his wife were country folks
but the Lord had laid His hand on Adolfo and wherever he went
he talked to everyone about becoming a Christian. He seldom
wore shoes and my conclusion was that early in his ministry he
couldn't afford to buy any, and then later, as his feet got
calloused and he was accustomed to the rural trails with their
sticks and stones, he felt more comfortable barefooted. Surely the
church in Retalhuleu could have afforded to give him a pair, for it
was the largest church on the Pacific coast of Guatemala with
several hundred members and many satellite congregations,
which were organized into churches under his leadership.

Don Adolfo soon gained a reputation as the barefoot
preacher who ended a conversation by inviting one to become a
Christian. That is not to say that his boldness was repulsive, for
he was such a sweet man and so committed to Christ that
everyone loved him and would always stop to listen to what he
had to say about the Gospel. Don Adolfo and his wife had one
daughter, and had seen to it that she was well educated. She was

principal of a large school in town and very capable. She was active in the church and had married one of the young men who wanted to follow in the footsteps of his father-in-law, but somehow just didn't have the same gift of evangelism. But he was motivated and always attended our rural seminars for training new pastors and was faithful in reading the assignments and doing his homework. Yet he never seemed to pass the examinations the Presbytery required for ordination. I often had fellowship with don Adolfo, and like everyone else, I adored the man. Several times, I visited his church where he always asked me to preach or teach and I was blessed just to be there and take part in his lengthy services.

The Synod meeting was a yearly gathering of all the Presbyterian pastors and elders of Guatemala. For a couple of hours each morning they heard reports and prayed for the work and the pastors of each church. But no one thought of these meetings as business meetings, and called them conferences. Each church wanted to have the Synod meeting in its town because it was a weeklong evangelistic campaign. It was a great attraction and many leaders of Synod attending meant good preaching each evening at no cost to the local congregation. Many spent the afternoons visiting in the homes and inviting people to come out that evening. It was kind of like having Billy Graham visit your town and bringing all his staff who would help direct long prayer meetings at daybreak and then preach in the evening. The Synod meetings generated great enthusiasm for the Gospel and growth for the church.

The first time I attended one of these Synod meetings was in Retalhuleu where don Adolfo was pastor. This was my first year in Guatemala, and I was new to the customs and programs that had been part of the Church for several years. Don Adolfo Martinez wanted to help me become part of the ministry there so he asked me to give the altar call after the preaching on one of the nights. They had brought in a special preacher from Mexico and he was very good and knew how to encourage people to listen and respond to the Gospel. These meetings were long and exciting. Before the two to three hour service ended everyone was enthusiastic and responsive. So it was a real privilege to be invited to give the altar call. Since this was new to me, I used some of the standard types of invitations that I had learned in meetings in the States including what I had seen Billy Graham use in his crusade in Los Angeles. I had also been part of inviting the youth to come to Christ in our summer camps and Christian Endeavor conventions. But this was different. The crowd was not familiar with my quiet Presbyterian manner and hardly responded. Alfredo was not very happy with the response and soon jumped to his feet, pushed me aside and started his own brand of demanding that everyone come forward. Of course, with his experience with those folks, and his enthusiasm, he was very successful and a large number of folks came forward with his urging.

The attendance in this tropical town was so great they rented an open air dance hall that held about 1,500 people. All the benches from the church were not nearly enough so they begged, borrowed and rented every bench in town whether from city hall, dance halls or homes. They were able to gather enough so that most everyone was able to sit down during the meetings. These same benches became a bed at night and if you got there in time, you could claim one and not have to sleep on the cement floor. Most of the families in the extended area came for the week and slept in the hall and the church provided the meals. There was great fellowship and outreach that resembled the old-fashioned revival meetings of the early days in the United States.

My problem was that I was late to the hall one night, having had to chair a committee meeting. When I finally arrived at the improvised dance hall, not only were the lights out, but all the benches were taken and many people were sleeping on the floor on their straw mats called *petates*. I had come prepared with a sleeping bag, but I had hoped to be able to get something off the floor. No such luck, in fact when I started moving around among the sleeping delegates, the only space I found large enough for my sleeping bag was right in front of the pulpit. The hard cement floor was clean but not very comfortable, but I soon managed to get to sleep. About 4:00 in the morning, long before it was light, I was awakened with singing. I pulled back the cover of the sleeping bag to find that everyone was up, dressed and had arranged the benches in their proper places. The singing was the beginning of the early prayer meeting! Here I was, right down on the floor in front of the pulpit. They had ignored me, cleaned up the area and started the service in spite of a missionary asleep right there in the middle of everything. I can't imagine how I managed to sleep through all the commotion, but there I was in my pajamas, looking out of my sleeping bag wondering how I could get dressed and roll up the bag right there in front of everyone. Fortunately my trousers were right beside the bag and I managed to put them on over my pajamas while inside the bag. Everyone was so polite and discreet and pretended not to notice me, and went right on with their singing and praying.

Alfredo's Bible is Chopped Up
Chanutla, Guatemala, 1953

Don Alfredo Mazariegos, a young pastor just out of
seminary, was so thrilled with what God had done in his life that
he walked from village to village, over the dusty roads stopping
anyone who would listen simply to tell them about Jesus and the
changes that He had made in this new believer's life after
becoming a Christian. One day he convinced a few elders to join
him on foot and preach to the peasants in the small village of
Chanutla. They arrived about dusk, and found a good site in the
plaza and public marketplace where they could preach and pass
out small portions of the book of John which told of the miracle
of the new birth. Next they went up and down the dusty streets
inviting people to come and hear about Jesus. But it was not to
be. No sooner had they started to sing and preach than the Roman
Catholic Church bells began to ring and a gang of enraged men
started after them with machetes flying. The small group of
evangelists had to run for their lives. In the scramble, don
Alfredo's precious Bible slipped through his fingers and he didn't
dare go back to pick it up.

When they were a safe distance, they turned to look back. The men were taking their rage out on his precious Bible. They were gleefully chopping it to pieces with their machetes, swearing and shouting, in Spanish, "kill the *protestantes*, kill the protestants."

Alfredo reflected a spirit of humility and love for his people throughout his life. When he was in seminary his vacation assignment was to visit the *ranchos* near the town of El Rancho. This is a small village in the northeastern area of Guatemala. It is a hot, dry spot along the road to the port city of San Jose. The town of El Rancho is one of the first places our Mission began work in Guatemala over a hundred years ago. Before there were roads it was reached by steam railroad and was easy to get to. Consequently, the missionaries quickly chose this area and began establishing a church there. Now most of the village is Christian, and the leaders have often invited seminary students to spend their summer with them to visit the members and the villages nearby. The elders provided a place in a back room of the church where Alfredo could sleep and the ladies of the congregation took turns inviting him to their homes for meals. The meals were simple and consisted of black beans, tortillas and coffee. This is the normal menu for the area and Alfredo was happy with the arrangements.

The elders asked him to teach the Sunday School class and preach on Sunday evenings. These evenings were dedicated to holding the regular Evangelistic meetings. He was also assigned the preaching at the weekly prayer meeting. During the week, he was to visit the homes of the members and also the nearby villages to invite people to come to Christ. Most of the villages are on the river because the hot valley is dry and semi-desert. But Alfredo was so enthusiastic about winning folks to Christ he often took off into the hills even in the heat of the day. He was always seeking out people who did not know Christ. I still remember visiting El Rancho one afternoon and there was Alfredo just coming back from a long hike up into the cactus covered hill country, waving his sombrero to cool his hot brow. He had spent the whole day evangelizing the rural *campesinos* and talking to them of Christ. Of course, he helped them some with their work and his countenance showed he had had a tough day. My thought at the time was, what a crown he will have when God calls him home and says, "Well done thou good and faithful servant; enter thou into the joy of thy Lord." How humbling it was to realize that his heavenly crown would be so much more beautiful than mine. I traveled in a car, had soft drinks for refreshment when the heat was too much for me, and I could go home to a comfortable bed at night. Alfredo never knew such luxury in this life.

He was soon called to a small church in Guatemala City. God used his spare time to continue his studies and after many years of night classes he not only finished high school, but studied in the University. He married a wonderful Christian girl and raised a godly family. He often invited us to his humble home and served us a delicious dinner. When Dr. Richard Halverson, pastor of Fourth Church of Washington DC and later Chaplain of the US Senate, asked us to host a work team one summer, don Alfredo graciously gave the fellows his study and laid some borrowed mattresses on the floor so they could stay with him, eat his food, and work in his church. It was a most wonderful time, both for the church and for the work team. The university students experienced the simple lifestyle and the gracious love of don Alfredo and his family. And the Church glowed in the opportunity to serve and love the *gringos*. Don Alfredo was secretly suspicious of the *Norteamericanos* because of what he had been taught by some of the communist professors at the university. Now he had the opportunity to find out firsthand what dedicated Christian fellows from the North really felt and thought when they became Christians.

God used this man to be a giant in establishing the Gospel in Guatemala. It was an honor to have him as a close personal friend in Christ.

Saved by a Miracle

La Estancia De La Virgen, Guatemala, 1953

I was to preach in a small church in one of the barrios of Guatemala City and sat in the adult Sunday school class before the worship service to get a feel for who was there and where the class was headed. The discussion was on miracles. The theme was a current event in the whole country for it seemed that everywhere people were being killed by the guerilla forces. As the discussion became more and more serious, they began to look for theological justification for seeking a change in government and whether the Christians should pray for a miracle or support the guerilla movement as a biblical way to get justice. One opinion was that the people had to take part with the rebels in order to change a corrupt government. The other opinion was that as Christians we had no right to participate in politics.

As the discussion heated up, a visitor seemed to be quite agitated and kept trying to interrupt the teacher. Most teachers in these smaller churches do not permit discussion but concentrate on the outline guide, feeling it is more important to get the lesson finished than discussing the truth being taught. It is not usually allowed because one never knows what the visitor will say and what might come up that has nothing to do with the biblical passage. They just have to finish the lesson guide before the bell rings and class is over. Finally, the teacher realized that he was going to have to let the visitor speak.

Actually, the visitor did not want to express an opinion but rather he had quite a story to tell. He stood up as though to give emphasis to what he wanted to say. After a pause and a hem and haw he said:

"I have had a first-hand experience with the guerillas in the mountains of Cobán, for I live in the village of La Estancia de la Virgen. My name is Pedro and I am an elder in the Presbyterian church there. The members can vouch for what I am going to say. We are a poor village and most of the families have a small hut in the village but have to go up into the mountains to plant corn and beans on a small plot of ground we have carved out of the grass and trees. My plot is about as far away as any and I have to spend a long time to get there and then work all day in the hot sun just to feed my large family.

"One day I was hoeing the corn and planting some more

beans when a group of men with machine guns showed at the edge of the forest. They pointed their guns at me and demanded that I come over to where they stood. They obviously didn't want to be seen in the open. Knowing what a danger I was in, I prayed a silent prayer for safety and then walked slowly over to where they stood. Their attitude and fatigue clothing made it clear they were part of one of the so-called communist guerilla movements that were trying to overthrow the government. I confess I was afraid!

"They quickly tied my hands behind my back and put a gag in my mouth. They then told me that the boss had ordered that some of the farmers were to be taken hostage and I was the most available. I knew my life was in grave danger because we were very poor and my family would not be able to raise a ransom to buy my liberty. Of course, the only thing my family and the people in the village would know was that I had disappeared. Then later they would receive the ransom note asking for a huge sum of money. I suppose that the guerillas hoped that the church people or the mission would find the money somehow and buy my freedom.

"I was not beaten nor treated badly, but they were strong and firm and their guns dictated that I obey, which I did at once. However, I had a secret weapon they knew nothing about. I could pray and I knew the church would have an all-night prayer meeting as soon as they realized I was missing. This had happened before and the church was experienced in praying for its people who were sick or in trouble.

"We started off along the trail that led into the mountains of Cobán and I realized that we were headed for their secret hideout and that maybe they would kill me. As I was led way back into the forest, I prayed harder knowing what was ahead of me because of the stories that were circulating about their willingness to kill anyone who would not cooperate with their cause.

"I was scared, I can tell you, and began to silently pray more fervently! Just at that moment one of the leaders came to help them with their new prisoner. He took off his helmet and gave me a good look. 'What are you guys doing with Francisco?' he demanded. 'He is a friend of mine from the church in town. Release him at once and send him back to his corn field!'

"Trust me - I believe in miracles!" he said, and then he sat down. There was silence in the whole room for a few minutes and then the teacher asked the class to pray for Pedro and for his pueblo. I realized afterward that they never did solve the problem of what is the best way to get a change of government, but they were convinced by his testimony that God does work miracles for his people in any and all circumstances!

"Who shall separate us from the love of Christ? Shall tribulation, or distress, or persecution, or famine, or nakedness, or peril, or sword? As it is written, For thy sake we are killed all the daylong; we are accounted as sheep for the slaughter. Nay, in all these things we are more than conquerors through him that loved us. For I am persuaded, that neither death, nor life, nor angels, nor principalities, nor powers, nor things present, nor things to come, nor height, nor depth, nor any other creature, shall be able to separate us from the love of God, which is in Christ Jesus our Lord." Romans 8:35-39

A Bandit is Converted to Christ
Santa Maria, Guatemala, 1953

Dr. Edward Haymaker, pioneer missionary to Guatemala in the late 20th century, had this criteria for his work: "If we are to win the Guatemalans to Christ, we must teach them the seriousness of sin, the kindness of God and the unspeakable love of the Father." This true story of Oscar Barrientos' conversion shows how these Divine Imperatives led him to face up to his life of sin and, by the grace of God, open his heart to the Lord. Discovering how much God hated sin moved Don Oscar to realize how much he needed God who would provide him with eternal forgiveness. Here is how I heard his story:

We were holding a retreat for the youth of Bethel Church in Quetzaltenango. Don Pablo, who is an active leader in the church offered to loan us the building at his coffee *finca* in Santa Maria which was about 10 miles away. It was not a large place and had no furniture, but the young people were thrilled to be the first to attend the first retreat the church had ever had. The kids had to do the cooking outdoors over an open fire but that was no problem because cooking black beans and heating tortillas can be done almost anywhere.

Don Oscar Barrientos, the pastor of the church, was invited to speak to the youth the first evening. We wanted to draw them closer to the church, establish a good rapport with him, and help them see him as a spiritual leader of the youth and not just of the older adults. Youth are not always appreciative of their pastor. We were gathered around an evening campfire and I was very surprised that he chose to tell them about his youth instead of preaching a sermon, but it was the right way to make a hit with them, and it was the beginning of a new relationship between don Oscar and the church.

As he got up to speak I saw a flash in his eyes. Then he told us this story: "My father was a *pistolero*, (bandit with pistol) and quite famous because he was so accurate he could shoot through the neck of a bottle and the bullet would come out the bottom." He told us that his father's greatest goal in life was to be a revolutionary and lead a coup that would overthrow the government of Guatemala. He taught his boys his hatred of the oppression of the present dictator, a perpetrator of many of the injustices toward the people. Don Oscar's father also hated religion. He claimed that in his youth his experience with the Roman Catholic Church had been only deception, hard discipline, and rules. As a youth, this turned him against the church instead of winning him to its sacred life. Don Oscar said that his father had observed the priests taking advantage of the young girls and used the confessional to convince them that they should submit to their advances. He saw other injustices such as demanding money from the rich so it could be given to the poor, who never saw a penny of it. The religion he described was certainly religious but resulted in anything but a Christian example. He described it as a show of pomp, robes and authority, especially in the rural churches. In revenge one day, at gun point, don Oscar's father ordered the priest of the local perish to come to their *finca* and baptize a dog.

Don Oscar readily followed in his father's footsteps, and also became the leader of a revolutionary group that sneaked over into El Salvador at night to harass the authorities. From the southern border of Guatemala, where they lived, it was easy to slip across the border at night and then flee back when they were about to be caught. Now don Oscar had a price on his head and the Salvadoran Army tried every way possible to catch him. He was safe as long as he was on the Guatemalan side of the border and was careful to stay there.

However, he was a rebellious youth and quickly bored. It wasn't long until he and his gang started an insurrection in Guatemala. As youth they were ready to fight for justice anywhere. They were soon caught because they were wanted both in El Salvador and in Guatemala and there was no way to avoid the authorities. They were arrested as bandits and revolutionaries and condemned to prison. They were locked up in the penitentiary in Guatemala City.

All three of the gang decided to try to escape, and planned a daring attempt by climbing over the 15 foot wall of the prison. One was shot and killed just as he reached the top; don Oscar and his other pal dropped down to the ground on the outside and ran toward freedom. But the guards saw them escaping, and as they ran down the sidewalk the soldiers shot and killed his pal. This penitentiary was in the center of the city so the guards had to be careful where they aimed their guns so as not shoot an innocent victim. Don Oscar's life was saved because just as the guards were about to pull the trigger a lady stepped out of the door of her house that opened onto the street. They could not shoot without hitting her. He quickly ducked around the corner and escaped. From there he made his way at night down into the arid desert area of Zacapa which is near where he grew up and close to the Salvadoran border.

He was hunted by the authorities so he couldn't stay in Guatemala nor could he go into El Salvador, where he was also wanted. After several days without anything to eat or drink the heat was taking its toll. The heat, the loss of his pals, and having nowhere to turn, made him despondent. He finally decided that life wasn't worth living any more. He was wanted in both countries and had no way to escape. The moment he showed his face he would be captured and shot. He finally sat down under a desert bush for the little shade it would give him and put his gun into his mouth to kill himself, just as his father had killed himself.

Unknowingly, he was near a palm covered hut and as he was about to pull the trigger, he heard a lady singing *"Cristo me ama,"* the children's chorus that says "Jesus loves me this I know." It was such a sweet voice and so very sincere that he stopped to listen to all the verses. It was a message that he had never heard before. Slowly he took the gun out of his mouth, uncocked it, and just listened. When she finished singing he slowly worked his way over to her little palm hut. She stopped her daily chores and turned to see who was coming. The lady of the house greeted him warmly and offered him some *chicha*, a drink made from sugarcane juice and cold water, for she could see he was very hot and tired, hungry, and despondent. It tasted so good. She invited him to sit down in the shade of the hut to drink his *chicha*. He asked her who was this Jesus she was singing about. Very simply, she told him of Jesus' love and how He had saved her and changed her life. She and her family were very poor but still happy, and the heat and poverty of living in the dry barren area of Zacapa was only temporary for them, for God had a mansion, with streams of living water, fruit trees, and fresh cool breezes prepared for them in heaven. As she shared her experiences as a Christian, don Oscar found that it was just what he needed and begged her to help him become a Christian, too.

After this conversion, a few years passed and both countries had a change of government and forgot all about him and he was no longer a fugitive. Don Oscar went over to the Friends Mission in Chiqimula and discovered they had a Bible School and would take him in and give him board and room. The mission had many young people who were preparing for the ministry in this school. He studied there, learned to pray and got so excited about his new faith that he soon wanted to share his testimony with everyone. He began teaching Sunday school in the small churches in the Zacapa area. It was there that he got his training and experience to go into the ministry. He went out preaching and sharing with those country people the great change that God had made in his life. As he developed his skills he was called to larger and larger churches. Eventually he was called to be the pastor of the Presbyterian Church in Quetzaltenango.

When Esther and I were assigned there in 1950 we met this man of God. He was just a native pastor to us, but loveable and wanted our help, so we became close friends. I think our prayer times together were some of the most precious experiences I ever had in Guatemala. The young people only knew him as *Reverendo* Oscar Barrientos, an older man that occupied the pulpit every Sunday. Listening to his testimony that night, they discovered the difference between a youth with a revolutionary spirit and a youth dedicated to living his whole life for Christ.

Don Oscar was a great evangelist and a deeply spiritual man. He was not ashamed to shed a few tears as he talked with the youth that night, sharing how his own youth had been spent in sin. He told how he now rejoiced in the new life God had given him.

As He Drew His Pistol
El Rancho, Guatemala, 1953

Don Oscar was pastor of Bethel Church on the plaza, which was quite influential because many teachers and community leaders were members. He lived next door to Esther and me and we soon became close friends. We felt a common bond in the ministry. He asked me to take charge of the youth program and so we often got together to discuss the Lord's work and prayed together over the problems and activities of the church. He had little experience with men's programs so we introduced a men's fellowship program. The fellowship included a Saturday breakfast once a month in their homes. We often had as many as 50 men come out for tortillas, beans and coffee. This same group wanted to have an early prayer meeting in their homes which soon became a major part of the ministry of the church. Each Saturday we met about 6 a.m. in different homes before the men went to work. Being at 8000 ft altitude it was very cold in the winter. There was no heat in the homes so I wore my heavy overcoat but still had chills as we knelt on those cold cement floors. I don't recall a single home that had a carpet. In our home, Esther and I had placed a native blanket on the floor in front of the fireplace to make it more homey but visitors from the Church always walked around it and wondered what it was doing on the floor.

I love this story that don Oscar shared with me about 1952. In his younger days he was the pastor of the small country church at El Rancho. El Rancho is in a very dry area on the Caribbean side of the country and considered by most to be the desert of Guatemala. Most of the water comes from the Motagua River. They cannot afford pumps to water their gardens and orchards so the only vegetation is along the banks of the river. Rev. Barrientos tells of the conversion of one of the revolutionaries in the area. This *bandido* always carried his *pistola* even after his conversion, and the authorities and citizens were afraid of him for he had killed several people before coming to know the Lord. He took very seriously the destiny of anyone who was lost in sin and needed salvation in Jesus Christ. This *bandido* had been thoroughly converted, and evangelized everyone who would listen to him. As he talked to people about their need to become a Christian, he would let his coat come open so they could see the handle of his gun. Naturally they listened because of his reputation as a *pistolero* and excellent shot.

Don Oscar had built up the enthusiasm of the congregation to hold a series of evangelistic meetings and the congregation had been much in prayer that many would accept Jesus Christ. That Sunday the church was full. We don't know how many the *bandido* encouraged to attend by telling them of God's threat of damnation, and a view of his pistol at hand. His enthusiasm was running high. The whole service was very loud and enthusiastic with lots of hymns and testimonies. One of the most interesting testimonies was given by the *bandido* himself who told of his past life as a criminal and how Christ had brought about great changes in his way of life. Now he desired that everyone come to know Christ as Savior and to experience the new life in Christ just as he had. When the altar call was given, one or two stood up to accept Christ, but the response was slow. However, the enthusiasm of the *bandido* ran high and he wanted to see everyone become a Christian. In desperation he finally jumped to his feet, took out his gun and shot several times through the roof of the church and then commanded everyone to stand up, go forward, and accept Christ. In a loud voice he shouted out that everyone had to accept Christ and become a Christian right on the spot. The pistol made it obvious that there would be dire consequences for those who did not respond. Don Oscar reported that this same *bandido* saw to it that every church member lived out their faith every day. He simply strutted around town with his pistol clearly at the ready.

Do You Believe in Miracles?
Don Javier Does
Palín, Guatemala, 1965

Don Javier is one of our Mayan Indian pastors in Guatemala. He is a very ardent believer in miracles because he lives by them. He was pastor of the small church in Palín, a town that is famous for its outdoor market which is held weekly under a huge ficus tree planted by the Spaniards in the early days. A similar tree was planted in the plaza of most of the towns established in Guatemala by the Spanish Conquistadores. When they settled the country in the 1500s, they built a church and military barracks as the center of each pueblo they established.

Don Javier was called to be the pastor of the small Presbyterian church in the village sometime in the 1960s. But it was a small town and the church did not have enough members to support him, much less keep the manse in good condition. When the San Mateo Presbyterian Church of California offered to send a work team to help us, I asked don Javier if there was something they could do for him. Don Javier was very excited for this was an answer to the prayer of the congregation. The town is near Monte Sión and the team lived there in the faculty cabin that has nice beds and flush toilets and we provided meals for them. The team not only repaired the manse but visited outlying areas where don Javier had established small congregations. The team gave their testimonies and shared in their evening services after they had worked all day on the manse and the small church building. It was a very wonderful experience for all of them.

The team fell in love with don Javier. His testimony and ardent love for the Lord and the people was very contagious as they watched him share the gospel with the farmers around Palín. Another team, from InterVarsity Christian Fellowship, that used Monte Sión for a summer work project, also got to know don Javier and his love for the Lord. He was so helpful that the team invited him to attend the next Urbana missions conference to be held in Champagne, Illinois. Of course he accepted even though he did not speak English or have a dime to his name. He simply told us, "God will provide just as He has always done."

The InterVarsity work team in Guatemala that year had a vision for missions. They wanted the other students at the conference to hear don Javier's testimony, use his testimony for helping tell about missions, and just to mix with the college students as they learned about missions. So they took a collection to pay his airfare to the USA and care for him while in Urbana. When the church in San Mateo, California heard that don Javier was to be at the conference some of them offered to meet him there and do what they could to make his visit a success. By the time they all got together at the missions conference they were sure that don Javier should come and visit them in California too. At once don Javier accepted the invitation because he had a sister living in Los Angeles and he was delighted with the prospect of going to visit her. But there were no funds to pay for his travel to California. As usual, he accepted on faith and told them God would provide a way to get there. So it was settled, although some of the students did not believe that the plans would mature for they could not see where the funds were coming from!

The days of the conference were just about over and one of the students asked him how he was ever going to get to California. After all, he had absolutely no money. How could a Guatemalan pastor who made only about 25 dollars a month buy tickets from Illinois to California? His answer to the student was short and to the point. God will provide! The last day of the conference arrived and he had no prospects. That was when a stranger came to don Javier and asked him if he wanted to accompany him in the long drive to California. "What a miracle" don Javier remarked to his student friends. "But, how did you know a ride would be provided for you?" With his typical faith attitude don Javier answered, "Why, it's just what I expected Him to do. God has always provided for me!"

YOUTH WORK

Assigned to Youth Work
Quetzaltenango, Guatemala, 1951

Esther, Peggy, and I arrived in Guatemala in 1950. We had been transferred from Colombia, South America because the Board of Foreign Missions wanted Esther to have an ophthalmologist who was a diplomate of the Ophthalmology Association to care for her eyes. In fact that was the only choice, otherwise we would have to give up being missionaries and return to the States. We found that Dr. Quevedo of Guatemala was an excellent doctor and had studied in the States. The missionaries of Guatemala, led by Stan and Betty Wick and Bob and Bernice Thorp, quickly agreed that they would like us to become members of their mission and encouraged the rest of the personnel to approve our becoming members of the Guatemalan Mission. We had been classmates in seminary with Bob and got to know Bernice, Stan and Betty at language school in Medellín, Colombia, where we all studied Spanish in preparation for our work in Latin America.

Upon arrival in Guatemala, we were assigned to the city of Quetzaltenango to live in an old missionary house that was vacant. Harry and Rosenda Peters had lived there but had asked for a transfer to another field for they believed that the church in Guatemala was well established and they wanted a new and more challenging assignment where they could do church planting and evangelism. That old missionary residence needed new bathroom fixtures and a better water supply but the executive committee was reluctant to put money into a house that was vacant.

The Peters had worked with the churches along the Pacific coast of Guatemala in the area known as Suchitipeque and Pacific Presbyteries. Since we arrived soon after they left and lived in their house, the Guatemalans assumed that we were to take their place and work assignment. Many of the coastal churches couldn't afford a full time pastor and so a missionary was assigned to preach monthly, serve communion once a quarter and moderate the sessions of those churches. But Morrie Morrison, director of the La Patria School, wanted someone to work with the high school students and help in their sports program. Dudley and Dorothy Peck, who worked with the Mam Indians, wanted someone to take over their responsibilities to the Spanish speaking people in the coffee *fincas* where a large number of workers had never been evangelized. The English-speaking families at the United Fruit Company plantation in Tiquizate needed a missionary to preach once a month to their English-speaking congregation. The two Presbyterian churches in the pueblo had large memberships. They were able to pay full time pastors but still the missionaries who preached at the English service in the morning were also expected to visit at least one of the Spanish congregations in the evening, encourage their pastor, and preach in Spanish. So I had a full schedule before I even arrived.

All of the missionaries of Western Guatemala had more to do than time permitted. Don Pablo and doña Dora Burgess were working among the native Maya Quiché people and their churches. She was translating the Bible into the Quiché language. Dudley and Dorothy Peck built the Mam Center to minister to the Mam-speaking Mayans, another large tribe, and were very busy with a clinic and translation of the Bible into that language. However Dudley took time to visit the coffee *fincas* on the western slopes of the volcanoes of the area. Miss Morrison had developed a large and famous mission school with classes from kindergarten through high school. She had a real vision for these future leaders of the Guatemalan people. Today many are university professors or leaders in government. So for the first year we ended up working a little in each of these areas. Time quickly slipped by without a specific assignment, but we were happy and loved working with these people.

The Presbyterian Church in Quetzaltenango was quite large and influential and pastored by the Rev. Oscar Barrientos. We enjoyed working with him, Esther played the church organ and helped direct the choir, and he asked me to work with the *Esfuerzo Cristiana* (Christian Endeavor) youth group. One of the very special things that was started during our time there was the men's weekly prayer group that met twice a week, very early in the morning at the men's homes, before they left for work. They also had a fellowship breakfast once a month in one of their homes. I was very pleased that I had time to work with don Oscar and our prayer times kneeling on the front bench of the church during the week were very precious. It was a good relationship and we spent many hours together in discussions of the ministry and in prayer.

Don Oscar did not have much experience working with youth and asked me to be the sponsor of the youth program of the church. I loved getting to know the kids and working with the Sunday School where we trained them in the use of the newly translated Gospel Light Sunday school curriculum. Since we had worked with Christian Endeavor in California and had a background with the program, we brought lots of materials and ideas that were quite useful in training these young people. We soon found that they loved the idea of retreats and summer conferences so we had several. We also helped La Patria School set up a big rally in the City Opera House. It was a great success and we all were thrilled with the results.

During our second year in Quetzaltenango the missionary

sending agency of the Presbyterian Church in New York did a survey of the mission programs all over the world and decided that the next big thrust should be youth work. They asked each mission to assign one missionary full time to youth work. Since we still did not have a permanent assignment the lot fell to us, and our first major assignment was to organize youth programs in all of the 45 churches of the synod. We soon were very busy working with these three Presbyteries of Occidente, Pacifico and Suchitepéquez establishing *Esfuerzo Cristiana* in most of them. God blessed this program and soon there were youth societies in almost all of the churches.

We believed in the statement, "no youth program is successful without a Summer Conference program," which motivated finding places and inviting the youth to their first conferences and camping experience. There were weekend retreats at don Pablo's coffee *finca* in Santa Maria for the Quetzaltenango church youth and at San Jose el Higado in their church building for the youth of Suchitepéquez Presbytery. Mac Martinez and Tom Peterson from the Presbyterian church of San Jose, California, pastored by Dwight and Ruth Small, helped us in this first retreat. Our first weeklong camp was at Lake Atitlán where the mission owned a small lot and a vacation cottage. It was a very new and wonderful experience for them and a great success.

Esfuerzo Cristiana in Guatemala grew quickly and we found

ourselves spending more and more time in Guatemala City which was really the center of the Presbyterian Mission. A monthly youth magazine, called *El Esforzador*, was printed on a primitive mimeograph machine and mailed to hundreds of the youth. Soon we were under pressure to move to Guatemala City and assume the role of Superintendent of Youth Work of the Synod of Guatemala, which consisted of five presbyteries.

The next step was to organize week-long summer conferences for the youth of all five Presbyteries. The city fathers of Amatitlán agreed to rent us the city park for a week and since it was right on the shore of the lake, we had a wonderful setting. The park was a beautiful spot, with little dressing rooms with flagstone floors built right near the water, which the girls used as sleeping quarters. They reported that the floors were hard and uneven but they slept well. We rented a big tent for the guys. The 150 campers swam in the lake and there were rowboats to rent and lean-to caves for picnicking which we converted into an outdoor kitchen.

As we met the train, I was driving a new red convertible which, of course, became very popular. A couple of the youth who had ridden all day on that train from Western Guatemala to come to that camp later told me that they were on the train and planned to attend because a couple of cute girls in their village had invited them to come. They said it sounded like fun and being at the lake for a week convinced them to sign up. However, on the train they met some old buddies and had a couple of beers together and had decided to give up the camp and go on into

Guatemala City to spend the week with them. But when they saw me in a red convertible they changed their

minds and grabbed their suitcases and got off the train to join us. During the week, both of them came forward at the campfire and gave their lives to Jesus Christ. Their conversion was very real to them and they soon applied to attend the seminary and prepare for the ministry. We thank God for that night and their decision to give their lives to Christ. Today they both are in the ministry. One of them is the Guatemalan director of the conference grounds, Monte Sión, which we later purchased and built on the shore of that same lake.

We found a little amphitheater area near the park that we converted into a nightly campfire where we had testimonies, singing and sharing how to become a Christian. The speaker was from the seminary and gave an invitation each night for the campers to give their life to Christ. The seminary in Guatemala City had trained a quartet and these four fellows were a major part of the program.

One evening, just before dusk, we had the quartet and the

speaker row way out onto the lake without the campers' knowledge, then as we all gathered at the shore of the lake for the evening vespers, the quartet began to sing and slowly rowed into view. The campers were thrilled as they realized it was our leaders who were singing hymns and as the boat came closer to the shore they called out a greeting. The speaker then stood up in the rowboat and told us about Jesus who called some of the disciples on the shore of Lake Galilee. He then challenged the campers to dedicate their lives to following the Lord. As the preaching finished the speaker invited the youth to come to Jesus. He then explained that the quartet and speaker were all studying at the seminary so they could take the gospel to those who hadn't heard. He then asked if anyone wished to join them in their mission of preaching the Good News of Christ's death and resurrection. One very alert fellow was deeply moved and quickly jumped up and said, "Yes, I want to spend my life telling others." He waded out to the boat, climbed in, and left with them as they rowed off into the sunset.

A Camp with the Youth
of Quetzaltenango
Panajachel, Guatemala, 1951

The youth of
Guatemala had never
heard of a summer camp
and were very excited to
go to the first camp we
held at Lake Atitlán. The
camp was held at the
mission rest house on the
lake front which made it ideal, even though limited in space.
However, the first three days were filled with all kinds of
problems. One can expect that when one has about sixty campers
on a small lot with only a simple vacation house even though
there was the beach and lots of outdoor space. The campers were
used to the comforts of home and complained of anything and
everything.

The small three bedroom vacation house on the property had
only one bathroom so we built an outdoor latrine enclosed with
palm branches for the boys and let the girls line up for their turn
in the house. Most washed and bathed in the lake. The back porch
was very small but with an addition of a canvas roof we were

able to improvise a kitchen. The native cook surely did a superb job serving all of us three times a day from large pots placed over a wood fire. Each camper brought his own dishes so we didn't worry about dishwashing, and the lake was handy. It didn't take the campers long to discover that the sand on the beach made good scouring powder.

To provide sleeping quarters for the boys, we rented a small circus tent that provided room enough so that each could lay out his *petate* and blankets on the grass. Meetings were held on the shore of the lake and the same spot on the grass provided a great place for an evening campfire. Bible studies were held under the trees and the front porch was great for a dining room. The weather was nice so we could swim and bathe in the lake and be outside all day.

But the wind blew down the canvas we had put up for shade and kept putting out the wood cook fire. The nearby pueblo was not able to supply the great amount of meat and vegetables that we needed and no one was willing to make the thousand tortillas we needed every day. The sleeping tent came down on the men in the middle of the night and they had a hard time with the rustic bath room which consisted of a ten inch hole dug with a posthole digger. It was not long till they dubbed it *the target*.

A neighbor didn't like so many people around and one night turned the irrigation water into our lawn where we slept. The sixty campers and staff got so upset that the general atmosphere became one of criticism and complaining. When we played games, they forgot all about being good sports and playing fair. Two of the campers actually cheated several times trying to win the big prize of the day. One of the girls claimed that someone stole her jewelry from her bed roll and that was when the staff became desperate.

These many problems and conflicts drove the leaders and most of the campers to have several small group prayer meetings. They were the best kind of learning experience for all of us and God turned them into a blessing. The more mature youth from the church asked the campers to try loving as Jesus did, saying that this would turn into love and take the place of the bickering and accusations. Camping people talk about *teachable moments*, and we surely had found several for this camp. All of these things served to make us look anew to the Lord. There were private prayer meetings to ask for love and kindness and good attitudes at the games. Some ended in tears as we prayed in public for wisdom to work out the problem of the disappearing objects. These prayers were especially moving as young people who had never prayed in public before began to share their innermost feelings. These problems actually opened the door to a new spirit and the next day we could feel the presence of the Lord blessing the program with a new attitude among us all. The rest of the week this new spirit was referred to by several of the campers as *heavenly.*

Our program included a special campfire service the last night and each person shared a decision that they had made during the week. Some expressed having a difficult time speaking in public but were searching the scriptures for answers from God. Others related how they now looked at Christianity with new perspective. After most of the campers had placed a piece of wood on the fire and told of changes they felt God had made in their lives, we closed the service with a time of prayer. However, several stayed around the burning embers to talk privately to God. Some wanted to talk to a counselor and then placed a new piece of wood on the fire to express something they personally wanted to confirm or doubts to straighten out. In those sacred moments, several placed a stick on the fire to say they wanted to accept Christ as their Savior.

The same story was repeated with variations in El Rancho and Lake Amatitlán where we also held camps for the youth of those areas. In each one, the Lord gave great victory in their lives, and grace to live in a way that many of them had never before dreamed possible. Prayer proved to be the foundation for these great camping experiences. Before leaving for Lake Atitlán we had asked the men's society at the Church in Quetzaltenango to pray that God would meet these needs and lead the youth at the camp to turn their lives over to Christ. We felt that we were richly blessed by these conferences because of the faithful prayers of the men in our church.

Taking the Quartet to Cabricán
Cabricán, Guatemala, 1952

While Esther and I were in Quetzaltenango, the large Mission School, directed by Miss Morrison, called La Patria, asked me to develop a gospel team to represent the school. The fellows were quite talented and when I suggested they develop a quartet there was an enthusiastic response. In fact, the music teacher of the school was delighted to train them and get them ready for visiting churches and small congregations in the area. One of the members of the quartet was Wencheslau Xec, the son of a pastor who was helping Doña Dorothy Burgess on a translation of the Old Testament into the Quiché Language. Quetzaltenango is in the middle of the Mayan Indian towns and villages, so we were very welcome.

The most interesting invitation was on the Easter weekend. We had to go to the small village of Cabricán which was many miles into the cordillera of the Cuchumatanes mountains. My car did not have enough power to make the trip into that area and so I asked Stan Wick, a missionary to the Quiché people, if we could borrow his Jeep station wagon. He was as accommodating as usual, but there was one stipulation. We were not to take more than three people in the Jeep because one of the springs was broken and he was afraid the weight of more than that would break another spring. He said it was okay for all five of us on the paved road but when we got to San Carlos, where the paved road ended, he would allow only three. This part of the trip was over

steep, winding dirt roads with lots of pot holes. We had to accept his limited offer because there was no other transportation available. He suggested that when we got to San Carlos where the pavement ended, we could take the village bus or rent horses for the rest of the ten miles into that remote area.

We took our sleeping bags and left early, hoping to arrive in the early afternoon. All went well till we arrived at San Carlos. It was Good Friday and the rural people had been brought up with superstitions that prohibited doing any work on that most sacred religious holiday. There was no bus on Good Friday!

So we turned to our other alternative. We drove out to the edge of San Carlos and stopped at the first home to ask if they would rent us a couple of horses so two of the fellows could ride horseback and the other three of us would go in the Jeep. The plan was to toss a coin to see who would ride in the Jeep and who would go on horseback. They were actually looking forward to the experience. With high hopes, we stopped at the first home and, sure enough, there in the corral were a couple of fine horses. But it was Good Friday, the men were not working, and the horses were at home and "resting." I stopped the Jeep and one of the fellows who spoke the Mayan language went in to ask the great favor of renting us two horses for the weekend. In a few minutes, he came back with a long face. The horses were not for rent. Thinking they probably wanted more money, we obliged with a good offer. What we didn't know was that Good Friday was so very sacred that no one or his household would work for any price. Being very superstitions, the men not only took the day off, but their household absolutely had to take the day off, even their horses. We tried another home down the road and another and another with the same answer from each of them. No horses would be rented or allowed to work on Good Friday. This ended with the question: how were we to get to Cabricán with no horses and only three of the five permitted to ride in the Jeep? It was time for prayer, and it was done in Spanish, Mayan, and English. God surely would provide a way. We were on the King's business and going to preach and hold evangelistic meetings, but with no transportation in sight, we were beginning to get rather discouraged and frustrated.

It was too far to walk and at over 9,000 feet elevation, that was not feasible. Finally I asked if the fellows would share the walking. If they could take turns they only had to walk half the distance. Would they be willing? Since they had never had access to a car and did not know how to drive, I was the favored one who could ride all the way. They looked at each other and then asked me sheepishly what I meant. I suggested that we could leave two of the quartet right there and they could start walking. We three would drive a mile down the road and the other two would start walking from there while I would wait for the first two. By the time they arrived at the Jeep the other fellows would have walked their mile and I could take the first two up to that point and drop them off and pick up the second two and take them by Jeep another mile while they rested in the vehicle. After thinking about it, they decided there was no other alternative, so they reluctantly agreed. Mile after mile they half walked and half rode. It didn't seem long because they made a game out of it, and actually had fun checking up on each other. We finally arrived to be warmly greeted with warm *abrazos* and a cup of hot chocolate from the small group of folks in the church.

The meetings went well and the fellows sang beautifully, but the congregation was small and since there were no outsiders, there was not much point in giving an altar call. But the elder in charge of the congregation insisted, and we agreed that we must give the congregation the opportunity to accept Christ. I do not remember any decisions being made, but they all were impressed with the leadership of the youth and their enthusiasm, testimonies and love for the Lord.

Later I heard Dr. Dudley Peck tell a story about this

congregation in Cabricán. Dudley and Dorothy were the missionaries from San Juan Ostuncalco and directed the Mam Christian Center where they held weekly clinics for the people and organized a Mam Church. The church in Cabricán was an organized Presbyterian church and it had elders and deacons who actually ran the church. But it was very small and not able to support a pastor, so Dudley and Dorothy had been assigned as temporary pastors by the Presbytery. They made trips to the village every month to preach and train leaders of the congregation. The poverty of the people so moved them that on each visit Dorothy would bake a loaf of homemade bread for each family which they distributed after the evening service. Dudley explained that this helped to get people to come, but his conclusion was, "They learned to look out and around, instead of looking up!" He stated that this weakened his cause and many of them didn't really learn to be dedicated Christians or have a concern for the church, but rather they learned to look around to see what they could get.

La Patria School Gospel Team Visits Salcajá

Quetzaltenango, Guatemala, 1952

Evangelistic work has its blessings but also has its trials. A group of students from La Patria High School in Quetzaltenango decided to take Sunday afternoon to go to the village of Salcajá to sell portions of the Bible and give out tracts to the people there. The town has a small evangelical church which they used as the center of operations. This trip was especially difficult because they were asked to evangelize one on one, and sell Bibles on the streets in a town which already had a bad reputation for badly treating evangelists and resisting the gospel.

The quartet from the school claimed that this project was the most difficult they had ever been assigned. The members of this church had a reputation for being lukewarm and indifferent. The town also had a dislike for the gospel. The story is told of one of our early missionaries being stoned there for holding services in the plaza. Since other towns were more open to the gospel, the missionary work in that town had been neglected.

I still remember how reticent the school quartet was to go there that Sunday afternoon. They were fearful, knowing of the opposition to the gospel, and not many signed up. Those who went had to have a real conviction and desire that was not born of man. Nicolas, one of the students, came to me the day before they were to leave wanting to talk over their assignment. He had just learned that one of the residents of Salcajá had a grudge against the leader of the gospel team and he wanted to recommend that they cancel their visit. Naturally, the man who held this grudge would quickly share his feelings with his family and friends and try to get a gang ready to take it out on the team if it were to show up. We went to Professor Joaquin, the leader of the evangelistic group, and together we prayed about the possible danger and retaliation on the team. Then Joaquin declared, "I am still willing to go if the quartet will go with me."

Jacinto, the lead singer for the quartet, had responsibilities in his own church on Sunday morning so they were not able to leave until after lunch. The team was well equipped with portions of the Gospel of Luke and carried briefcases full of tracts. Two by two, they walked around town and talked to several people, offering them copies of the Gospel. Now, as in the past, the team could find no one who was interested in their visit or their tracts. Most people just jeered at them, or plainly cursed them saying, "We don't need any of that stuff in our town."

But the Lord had other plans and, as usual, there was a thrilling answer to their prayers. He is so good to fulfill His promises and often gives wisdom and a response we haven't anticipated. Joaquin and his partner noticed a group of men sitting on the ground gambling, and so he and his partner stood quietly by, looking over their shoulders, watching for an opportunity to break into the conversation. It was not long in coming, as one of the fellows soon ran out of money and started to leave, perhaps trying to cover his disgrace in losing. Jumping at the chance, they went over to him to show him a copy of the Gospel of Luke, and began to talk about its message of Jesus' birth. Due to some pre-conceived ideas about the Virgin Mary, they soon were in a heated conversation about the Bible. This interested the other men and they left their game to listen, and some even expressed their opinions. Soon a larger group had gathered there under the tree. The team led the conversation to Luke 7:37-50 and then passed out a copy of the gospel so each man could see for himself.

"It doesn't matter how bad a person you are, or what kind of sin you have committed, the Lord loves you and wants to know you personally," Joaquin told the group.

"Say, this is new to me," one man said, "I want to read more. How much is the booklet?" The others thought it was a good idea too and soon all the listeners had bought their gospels. Joaquin jokingly reported, "The sermon only lasted about 20 minutes but the men showed great interest and each one ended up with a copy. We are praying it will be read and will have a lasting effect."

As evening approached, the fellows started out for the church to make ready for the evening service at which they were to sing and give testimonies. Suddenly they were stopped by a fellow shouting at them from up the street. A bit fearful, they stopped to see what he wanted, not knowing if he was friend or foe. "Are you the guys who are selling those booklets?" he loudly asked as he drew near. Others gathered to see what the commotion and shouting was all about and the team began to really worry about what was to happen to them.

"Yes," they said timidly, "we have some booklets to sell, why?"

"Well, I want one too, that's good stuff." And so they were off on another selling campaign.

But they had more problems and the indifference they had received when they arrived accompanied them as they were ready to go home. After the evening church service, it was too late for bus service so they had to look for a taxi to take them back to Quetzaltenango several miles away. One of the church members had a car that he used for taxi service between Salcajá and Quetzaltenango, and they had hoped to get a ride back to the school with him. But it must have been too late because even when they offered him double the going rate, he told them he was not interested in making another trip that night.

However, the School Gospel Team quickly learned what it meant to let the Lord work out their problems. The quartet had to start out for home on foot. It was ten miles and they knew they would be reprimanded for being out so late, but there was school the next day and there was no alternative. That was not all, for they no sooner turned onto the main road than it began to rain, and hard. However, God was still with them, and as they huddled in a doorway for protection, Joaquin suggested they begin to sing the hymn, *I'm the Child of a King*. This was their last trial of the day, for just as they finished the chorus, an empty taxi, on its way to Quetzaltenango, came around the corner and gave them a ride all the way back to their dorms for only 10 cents apiece.

God Always Provides · · · Abundantly

Monte Sión, Guatemala, 1953

James 1:5 "He gives abundantly, without reproach."(KJV)

I marvel at the way the Lord touched the minds and hearts of many different people to help in the development of the Guatemalan Christian Camp and Retreat Center, Monte Sión. There were times when only a miracle could resolve a particular problem or lead in a particular part of the development. God led in the choice of a very special and appropriate place. He directed us to find the right plans and gave the knowledge to make the development of the site possible. He put us in contact with just the right people at the right time.

At first, we were denied the purchase of the property of our choice. This land was on the lake with a great view and the kind of privacy a camp needs. But Dr. Charles Ainsley, director of the American Hospital, told us he could not give his approval of this property because of malaria infestation all around the lake. He was a veteran missionary who had come to Guatemala years earlier to direct the medical program of the mission and that included looking after the health of the missionaries. He also built a medical practice that included the construction of the American Hospital in Guatemala City. He was one of the prominent leaders in the mission and had to give his approval of any project that dealt with the health of the missionaries and their work.

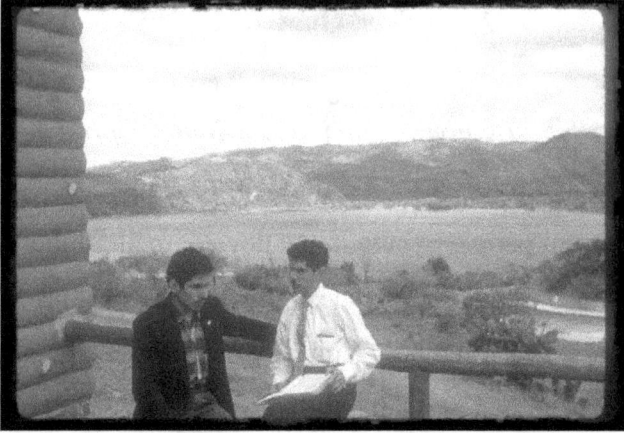

As he evaluated our plans for the new campsite we realized that Lake Amatitlán was in the zone of a major malaria infestation and shunned by most people. After a long search for the proper location for the new camp, we found what we considered the ideal property at a price we could afford. It was on a plateau overlooking the lake and possessed the other requisites for a perfect camp.

But when we proposed the purchase of this property to the executive committee, Dr. Ainsley very kindly and compassionately told me that he would have to vote against the purchase of this property because of the danger to the campers and missionaries. He assured me that he had long advocated for the mission purchasing and building a Christian Camp for the church, for he had made a decision as a youth at camp and strongly wanted us to have such a program in Guatemala. He offered his help in finding a different property and referred me to leaders in the government that could help me. Because of his reputation as the best surgeon in Guatemala, many important people and their families had been cured at our hospital and he had many good contacts. He even took me to look over the vacation property of the recently deposed dictator Rufino Barrios. It was a beautiful spot with lots of trees and a view overlooking Guatemala City. It was up for sale to settle some financial obligations of the family.

The price was right, the location excellent and it had something we could never have obtained on our own: electric lights installed, running water, and of all things, a telephone that was available only to the rich and government officials. But this property was not to be. It was on the old road to Antigua which had been replaced by a new paved highway so it was very isolated and we would be responsible for maintaining the old dirt road. This road was almost abandoned and constructed of dirt and gravel and poorly maintained. We were unable to get the approval of the Mission leaders at headquarters in the USA because they did not want the commitment of future dollars for the maintenance of this road. All this was quite a blow and we were getting very discouraged. Our project and dreams seemed to have all come to an end. First we were denied the beautiful and best property on the lake, with its great potential, and now this other property that had the utilities all installed had been vetoed by the officials of Mission Board in the USA.

Today we can see how God was in charge all the time and had better plans for the vision He had given us, but at that moment, we were quite discouraged. Our limited faith did not see that He was on the verge of providing more abundantly than we could ever envision because our present plans had suddenly come to a halt with a great big sign that read, *Road Closed*. How frustrated we became as the project came to what seemed like a final and permanent end. But God was not finished with us yet.

A year later, just before Mission Meeting, there was an article in the paper saying that the United Nations had sprayed the whole area around Lake Amatitlán with DDT. This miracle spray, developed during World War II, protected the armed forces all over the world. This spraying of the area around Lake Amatitlán was one of the projects the United States Government used to improve the health of many developing nations. It put an end to the danger of mosquitoes around the lake. Now the lake was malaria free. We went to Dr. Ainsley right away and told him of the article and reported the findings of the Ministry of Health of Guatemala. I think he rejoiced as much as we did. He gave his approval enthusiastically.

We went back to the property and found the owner hoeing his small corn crop. The site had not sold because no one wanted land that would not grow corn. The ground was actually hot in some places because of the steam vents from the nearby volcano. We were able to purchase about 50 acres at a bargain and gave God the glory for what is now Monte Sión Retreat and Conference Center. It is a beautiful site overlooking the lake with a great view of an active volcano in the distance. This defect, consisting of heat and steam vents, that made it unusable for farming made it ideal for a camp site. Recently an archeologist has confirmed that the site is a Mayan Indian temple site and full of artifacts more than 2000 years old.

A choice man of God and a dedicated saint was brought over from Cuba just as we closed escrow on the property, so he was present to preach the dedication sermon and lead in the communion service. This communion was part of the annual Pastors Retreat which was held in Guatemala City. The leaders accepted an invitation to the new property and this became the first contact of the pastors with the future retreat center. They took the bus down the 30 kilometers to the property so they could have a worship and dedication service seated in the empty field. Taking part in the dedication as an official act gave them a sense of ownership and a feeling that the retreat center was really theirs more than just a missionary vision. Their presence and sharing made them fully aware of the potential of the camp and their enthusiasm never died out. God had a way of providing the right people just at the right time to direct in the development and details of the new camp.

Here are just a few ways God provided for Monte Sión: He led Bill and Evelyn Boden to volunteer to come and help run the kitchen and care for the grounds. Tom Harnish was moved to get the hospital to provide a work car and give us used lumber which formed the skeleton for the lodge. God directed us to the plans for the lodge which were provided free by the US printing office. The Lord provided an engineer from the cement company to guide us in laying the proper forms and the donation of the ready mix cement for the foundation. He provided the flagstone for almost nothing when we were looking for a way to beautify and protect the buildings from the elements. So the story goes, on and on, for God was there every moment and directed each step of the planning and construction. Next, God sent us Chema, a native neighbor, who offered to look after the camp and do just any and all jobs at any time. The Ambassador of the USA to Guatemala and his wife were personally involved in the retreat center and encouraged the participation of the Union Church in Guatemala City. In his memory, they set up a memorial fund in the Ambassador's name that provided for the chapel. Later God sent many churches and work teams from the USA who prayed and shared in the development and construction of the buildings and site. Above all, Divine inspiration and guidance came from the leaders of Christian Camping International, through their conventions and visits, giving us technical direction and encouragement.

As we began the building of the lodge at Monte Sión we ran into all kinds of unanticipated problems which we now see were not problems but opportunities and definitely were blessings in disguise. When Esther and I were on furlough and did not know that we would soon be deeply involved in the building of the retreat center as part of our next assignment, God provided the plans for the lodge in a way that only God knows how to do. During our study in the States we discovered that the United States government provides bulletins written for the layman on just about every subject and most of them were either free, or cost less than a dollar. That was the year I was sent to Cornell University for a six week study course organized by the Agricultural Missions Organization. I met and studied under professors of the university teaching specialized courses for missionaries. These courses gave the background and knowledge in special areas that opened many doors. Then another few weeks were spent in Washington DC, where members of the Department of Agriculture taught us about subjects in our field of work and put us in touch with many resources. Among them was a master catalogue of government publications. This put us in touch with just the information that we needed to direct the construction of the camp lodge. The first step was to plan and build the lodge and we relied heavily on these plans for the buildings, plumbing, electrical installation and sanitary facilities.

Browsing through the master catalogue I found a plan and drawings for a camp lodge that was just what we had envisioned for Monte Sión. The plans were for a camp site in New York, but were exactly the same size and type of construction that we had envisioned for our site at the lake. The mission studied the plans and proposed location and enthusiastically gave their approval.

These plans and architectural drawings were the result of a research study by a student working on his doctorate in architecture where he compared all the camps in New York State. The title of the dissertation was, *The Ideal Camp*. This doctoral thesis was part of his research that included a questionnaire sent to over 100 camp directors in New York to determine what comprises the ideal camp. The thesis included what the director would include if doing the camp over and what they would eliminate if they were to create a new camp. It also included complete architectural plans for the ideal lodge and elaborate and detailed copies were made available to us for only $4.00. Needless to say, it didn't take me long to write out a check and send it off to the government's publication office. When we returned to Guatemala, we tucked the rolls of plans and details into the trunk of the car.

Furlough was over and we were anxious to return and begin construction of the lodge. We were just at the stage of drawing up a master plan for the newly purchased land, and I had to present detailed plans to the Mission Committee before starting construction. The doctoral thesis was based on a camp of about 150 campers. As we studied the plans and compared the youth program of our Guatemalan Church with the number of campers represented in the study of the architectural student, we found that they were almost exactly the same. What perfect timing! We were tempted to say *what a coincidence*, but later realized that it was God working in His usual way.

We found the ideal spot for the lodge with its dining room, kitchen, offices and meeting area at the center of the property and with a beautiful view. It was to have a fireplace for atmosphere and fellowship around the fire. It was to be large enough to feed 150 campers and it had to have a good kitchen and storage facilities for that number. This is exactly what this master plan by the architectural student laid out. But God had more for us. He humbled us further by moving that student to include in his basic plan all the necessary architectural drawings for the construction of the building. He laid out the basic floor plan, the size of the areas, the plumbing, electrical needs and how to lay them out, and the size of the timbers we were to use.

What an example of abundant provision. We had never imagined how abundantly God would resolve those insurmountable problems. That is when we discovered anew the abundant promise of James 1:5 "for he is always ready to give a bountiful supply of wisdom to all who ask him" (Living Letters, 1962) and I like to add, "just with the right timing so that it will work to His glory." He always adds what seems insignificant at the moment but which is necessary to make the promise complete. The Spanish translation of that verse says it this way, "He gives liberally without reproach." That is super abundantly. And that is just what happened to us. Now we had a place on the lake and a magnificent view and a property with rifts and hillocks which provided areas for all the different needs of a camp site. We wanted areas where we could separate the campfire from the activity centers and have it in a perfect setting for drawing apart. Later we discovered that the Tazaqualpa tribe of the Mayan culture had discovered this same site that God had prepared for us and had used it as their temple and worship center some 2,000 years ago. We actually found carved sacrifice stones, a temple site, a sacrifice stone where human sacrifices were probably performed and all kinds of equipment used for their worship of the stars, sticks and stones.

Soon it came time to start digging the trench for the foundation. But again, God was to test our faith. The choice site was at the top of the ridge. This would give the lodge a view of the whole camp and of the lake. The trench turned out to be right on the steam vents from Pacaya, a dormant volcano nearby. The deeper we dug into the soil to find a solid base for the cement foundation the softer and hotter the soil became. In dismay, I took a pick handle from one of the workmen and pushed it into the soil at the bottom of the trench to test the depth of the bad soil. With only the strength of one arm I was able to push the full length of the handle of the pick into the soft ground. The bottom of the trench, dug to receive the cement for the foundation of the building, was useless and had no strength to hold up such a large building. Now what would we do? It was time to stop and turn to the Lord again.

This new frustration and discouragement sent us to our knees. I think this was the first time that we ever considered taking a couple of days off in the middle of an important job and saying it was the Lord's leading. Esther and I escaped to a tourist hotel in Antigua for the weekend. Missionaries did not have the funds nor do they feel free to stay in these expensive tourist hotels. Most of our "sleeping out" was when we visited churches and slept on the floor or on rustic pine benches. We did go to the Antigua Hotel to eat lunch when we had visitors from the States, but no more than that. This time we were so frustrated and discouraged that Esther consented to our going there for a time of "getting away from it all" and getting our perspective back in order.

Again, God knew of our need, and sent the answer right to that tourist hotel. He wanted us to go there to rest and to get the answer to our problem. He had the answer right there waiting for us. The Antigua Hotel is built on the grounds of an old estate right in town and has a swimming pool, lovely gardens to stroll around, and warm fireplaces in the beautiful rooms, as well as delicious meals. There were hardly any tourists there that time of the year and we had lots of needed privacy. It was there that God put us in touch with a special couple that He had sent there precisely that weekend, just so we could meet them. In our conversation, he asked what we were doing in Guatemala, and specifically in Antigua. We explained that we were missionaries of the Presbyterian Church and our present assignment was youth work that included building a camp and retreat center for the Synod of Guatemala. Then I asked him if they were tourists and if they had seen all the ancient buildings of this first city of Central America established in1532 by Pedro Alvarado. His answer was so very profound and astonishing. He had been sent to Guatemala by his cement company to establish a ready-mix cement company called Mixto Listo, the first "ready-mix" company of Guatemala.

He then told us, "I am looking for a public relations project to gain the respect and reputation for this new ready mix company that will deliver cement already mixed to building sites in and near the city. I think your project is just what we are looking for. Could we donate the cement foundation for the lodge at Monte Sión?"

Do you believe in God answering prayer, *abundantly*? It didn't take us long to answer yes! But that is not all. I warned him of our dilemma of a soil that would not support the building. That was no problem for God; He moved the visitor to include in his offer the free services of the company engineer who would come and advise us how to resolve the soil problem. The engineer came to the camp the very next day, looked over our trench, and told us how to prepare the forms and how many iron re-bars of reinforcement the foundation would require in order to support the building. He provided the technical knowledge necessary to create a permanent, solid, foundation. ***God does answer prayer and He provides abundantly.***

Psalm 40, verses five and sixteen, "O Lord my God, many and many a time you have done great miracles for us, and we are ever in your thoughts. Who else can be compared with You. There is not time to tell of all your wonderful deeds . . . But may the joy of the Lord be given to everyone who loves Him and His salvation. May they constantly exclaim, ***"How great Thou art!"****(emphasis added)*

Monte Sión
Amatitlán, Guatemala, 1955

Psalm 87:1-3 *"His foundation is in the holy mountain. The Lord loveth the gates of Zion more than all the dwellings of Jacob. Glorious things are spoken of thee, O city of God. Selah."* *(KJV)*

Monte Sión was given its name by the Cuban Evangelist, Reverendo Martin Añorga when he preached the dedication sermon in the corn field on the new site. The Lord was definitely in the whole project and answered our prayers in marvelous ways. The Reverendo Añorga had been brought to Guatemala to lead the devotions and Bible study for the Pastors Retreat of the Presbyterian Church. The retreat was housed in an old missionary residence next door to Central Church in Guatemala City and the studies were in the sanctuary. One might say that it was coincidental that we purchased the site of Monte Sión on October 21, 1955, the same date as the Pastors Retreat, but we soon realized that God had planned it that way. God's timing meant that the missionaries in charge of the retreat, together with the pastors, caught the enthusiasm for a retreat program because God had planned both dates so that all could take part in the dedication and take communion right on the new property. We always had a special communion service at the Pastors Retreat so the leaders decided that the new Retreat Center was the right place to serve the *Holy Supper*. The culture of the Guatemalan Evangelical Church gives the communion service this lovely name. The day of the dedication, everyone got more and more excited about driving down to Lake Amatitlán for the afternoon. It was but a corn field at that time, yet God soon taught us that it was *holy ground*. It was a very solemn occasion.

Pastor Chema Duran was president of the Synod that year and we had often discussed with him our dream for a sacred spot where we could provide a Christian Retreat Center for camps, retreats and summer conferences for the youth. It would be a site for teacher training of the leaders of the church and especially help the youth establish a relationship with God. Many came to Monte Sión and there they surrendered their lives to the Lord of Lords. Some of them heard God's call to full-time Christian service while at one of the retreats.

Don Chema was very supportive, for he shared in our dream and was deeply concerned that the growing church should be a deeply consecrated church. We wanted to inspire the pastors to better serve Christ and the church and this conference center became a key element in this vision. We also wanted to challenge the youth in Christian living which could better be done in a sacred place where such an atmosphere would foster decisions to study His Word and seek His will for their lives as revealed by God's grace and love. A great emphasis was placed on teaching them how to study the Word. Another of our goals was to train pastors and church leaders in the use of the Scriptures in their pulpits, and in the homes of the members. One of the basic principles of our conference setting was to train church leaders in Christian Education.

The Mission also had a deep desire to help the elders and deacons to understand their responsibility for the growing church and how to reach their congregations more effectively. This conference center, with a good program, would help people to know when God was leading them to be pastors and missionaries. The motto of the retreat center would be to teach the great truths of the Bible and its basic principles, introducing the campers to the mind and heart of Christ by using outdoor teaching techniques, winning them to God, forming Christian character and training them for effective service for Christ and the Church.

The Synod elected a Board of Directors for Monte Sión which was united in wanting the Conference Center to fulfill these goals. The insignia has a Cross to stand for Salvation, a Bible to represent the concept of teaching the Holy Scriptures, and a campfire where decisions for Christ would take place. It was a day of celebration, for God had established Monte Sión with its foundation on this *Holy Mountain* in Guatemala.

Philosophy of Camping at Monte Sión
Lake Amatitlán, Guatemala, 1955

As the Retreat Site for the Presbyterian Camp in Guatemala began to take shape, there was a lot of discussion regarding the philosophy and program of the camp. We needed to convince the church leaders that we were going to help them with their work and ministry. The primary question they had was if this would help in winning the youth to Christ. The church also wanted the camping program to help them bring in new members and in turn help them grow into the likeness of Christ. This need and desire led us to design a program that would provide leadership training retreats. This is a translation of the document that was presented to the Guatemalan Synod for their approval:

> Jesus took his disciples on a Retreat that had a special setting on the shores of Lake Galilee. Jesus' retreat had seven campers and He met their special needs at this time apart. Jesus chose this spot on the shore of the lake so that He could speak to them privately in an intimate setting where He could meet those needs. This special setting lent itself to create an atmosphere where their thinking could be examined, challenged, and changed.
>
> One of Jesus' campers was a fisherman. He had become a leader of the group but later gave up this role when he was discouraged and exhausted. He expressed his desire to give it all up with these words, "I'm going back to fishing." Another two of the disciples were doubters. We know their names

because they are mentioned in the Gospels as Thomas and Nathaniel. They said they couldn't believe in Christianity unless they saw the risen Jesus in the flesh and could personally touch Him with their hands. They would not believe that Jesus was alive unless there was tangible proof. There were two others who were so busy they didn't have time for God. Their names were James and John and their priorities were all mixed up and they needed to get alone with the Lord. Peter was a very aggressive person and needed to have Jesus help him so God could change his attitude. He was prone to think that he didn't need God's help but could handle anything by himself in his own power. Just maybe Jesus could use him if he learned to realize he couldn't do it alone and would learn to depend on God. There were two more at that special retreat but we don't have their names, yet their need was just as great and urgent as all the rest. Each of these campers needed to take time to be alone with Jesus and let Him lead them into a deeper relationship and understanding of the Christian Life. They all needed to go on a retreat!

How did Jesus meet their needs at their little personal retreat with the Master? He reached out and touched Peter where he hurt. Peter was overconfident and had told Jesus that even if the others denied him, he would never do such a thing. That was the same night that he denied Jesus. He was warming his hands at a fire in the patio while Jesus stood before the Sanhedrin on trial for His life. That trial was a terrible mistrial and it meant that Jesus was giving up his life for us, but Peter didn't understand. When Peter was challenged by the maid who accused him of being one of them, Peter denied vehemently with the words, "I don't even know the man" and then cursed to prove he was different than the Jesus people.

Thomas and Nathaniel were very practical men, and they needed to have a very intimate conversation with Jesus that would lead them into a deeper understanding and relationship. They needed to understand that Jesus loved them much more than just temporal things. James and John were greatly saddened and they needed to see a real miracle, a miracle that would change their lives in a very personal way. All the disciples needed was to have time alone with the Master to review what was important in this life and how to trust in divine intervention. They didn't need preaching; they didn't need to go to church. What they needed was to be in a little group that could get away by the lake, away from their normal life activities. This had to be a place where the atmosphere would encourage them to open up to Jesus and where He could touch their lives in that very personal way.

Jesus set the example of the need for a Retreat Center where we can go aside alone to touch the Throne of Grace and to be prepared for the problems and temptations that Satan loves to put in our path. One of the best examples of Jesus' retreats was when He took time to be in the presence of God in preparation for that great temptation in the wilderness. This was a major trial, when he met the Devil, which consisted of those most serious series of temptations. Should He fail, the whole world would have been lost. (Matthew 4). Another example of Jesus "going aside" to come close to God, was the meeting on the Mount of Transfiguration. (Matthew 17).

Jesus used this same method when He had breakfast with the disciples at the Lake of Galilee. He took them aside so they could come closer to God and so He could talk to them about their future (John 21). He held a personal retreat according to Matthew 14 so they would be ready to "go up with His disciples" to His death. During His whole life He took time to be alone with God and now He was teaching His disciples to do the same.

Each of us needs these kinds of experiences. Some will call it a Conference, others will call it a Retreat, while still others think of it as a special all night Prayer Vigil. Our programs will be prepared to help the camper come to grips with his spiritual needs. This retreat that Jesus organized was a Breakfast by the Lake. It filled a serious need in the lives of the disciples. We will concentrate on retreats and conferences too because that is where the teaching of the Bible is so much more meaningful, when one listens more closely to what it says about our problems and sins. A Retreat is a time where we are caught up in a deeper relationship with God because there is an atmosphere that lets us discover that the Christian life is real and wonderful. It can become a time where we experience, "this is the way life should be." Our camping experiences can be like that. Monte Sión will be a time apart where we feel God's presence in such a way that we discover we always want that wonderful, joyful and happy relationship of being a Christian.

Perhaps it will be in a small group that talks about how to win over the many temptations of life. Others times one may say, "I accepted the Lord a long time ago, but I really needed this special time so I could know what following Jesus is all about." Our camp and retreat center must realize that a retreat is for building and molding lives to walk the Christian walk. The details of running a campground and maintaining the lawns and preparing the food is only a means to an end. It is such an important ministry because it is molding Christian life and character.

Camping should be an experience where youth are challenged to set high goals for themselves where they become highly motivated to bring Christ into every area of their lives and dedicate themselves to, "living for Him." It must provide a place where they can make those most important decisions of life: accept Jesus as Savior, choose a vocation that honors Him, establish Christian friendships or maybe meet their life partners. It is a time when one is led to decide what kind of a life partner God wants one to have. The camp will establish friendships, relationships and new thinking where attitudes toward drugs and other things that drag down life can be brought under control and plan a whole life where God takes control. These desires and needs must be settled by our youth before it is too late and they are caught up in the world's philosophy.

Youth must be provided with an atmosphere at camp where God can be seen in a proper perspective: a setting where there is an opportunity to ask questions about life in an atmosphere of being taken seriously and of being given Christian answers. It is a place where campers will learn to depend on the Scriptures and learn to enjoy studying them in depth so much that they will form the habit of studying them daily and decide to live by them. It must be an experience where prayer becomes so natural and real that they just talk to Jesus about anything, anywhere, anytime not only in church. It is so important that we help them in a setting where Christianity is real and lived out on a daily basis so they will learn to lay strong spiritual foundations that will last throughout their lifetimes.

A camping experience at Monte Sión is a time when the counselor looks for "teachable moments" when the camper may be open to the voice of God speaking. The spiritual atmosphere at camp opens the door to letting the inner voice speak to your heart. "But when the Holy Spirit controls our lives, He will produce this kind of fruit in us: love, joy, peace, patience, kindness, goodness, faithfulness, gentleness and self-control, and here there is no conflict with Jewish laws." (Galatians 5:22, translated from Spanish by author). These standards can become a reality when the camper sees just how practical they are and begins to realize how important it is to apply these things to one's life and heart.

New principles can be established and ideals and purposes for life can take on new meaning. A discovery of the love for God that is personal now becomes a reality, not only a biblical principle. As one learns how precious it is to spend time alone with God, maybe in the quiet of the early morning or a special place or setting such as their own personal rock or just leaning against a tree, the Quiet Hour becomes a precious lifelong habit. As one of our youth from a Christian school said, "Now I understand why it is so important to read the Bible alone." When they form new

Christian friendships, they form a whole new perspective of relationships that influences their whole life.

These activities at *Monte Sión* will come to life in programs such as: drama of My Heart Christ's Home, A Galilean Breakfast, Christian Outdoor Education Camps for the students who are studying at Christian schools, seminars on "Now I Know What You Mean When You Talk About Living For Christ," decisions like when Rigoberto says, "Now I understand why I should not pursue friendships with a certain girlfriend," discovering things like Bob Vernon's statement, "I live by principles so it is easy to make daily decisions off the cuff," camp themes like Don YoYo that illustrate how to deal with a super devastating ego and pride. Camping can schedule activities where one has to confront his own character flaws and as a result says to himself, "I was egotistical and I don't want to be like that."

Our camp program must teach and inspire the camper to establish spiritual goals for life where they are motivated to love the Scriptures and study them daily in devotion and prayer. As the groundwork is laid to establish correct attitudes toward self, life, and relationships to others, they learn how to meet temptations because their minds and hearts now know how to deal with sex, drugs, smoking, gangs, and other lifestyles that the world promotes. It is a time when they will come under the conscious leadership of Christ. As these things come under the umbrella of Christ, the camper is inspired to live for Christ, to love Him with all his heart, and love others as self.

This is the philosophy and mind of Monte Sión, Lake Amatitlán, Guatemala.

This was adopted by the synod and is the official guide to the Director of Monte Sión.

Enrique Makes a Decision
Monte Sión, Guatemala, 1958

At a youth conference at Monte Sión, a discussion had been
going on in the dorms in answer to a question one of the campers
had about why he couldn't have something he badly wanted. Was
it because his dad couldn't afford it or was it because God didn't
love him? That night we offered a drama instead of a sermon
because we felt it was a better way to help the campers
understand the meaning of surrender and how they could find
peace in their hearts. When confronted with the choice between
the world's materialistic life style and one that honored the living
Christ, they chose Christ.

The drama began on the stage in the lodge. Missionary Bob
Thorp gave an introduction based on Christ's statement in
Matthew 16:24-26, "If any man will come after me, let him deny
himself, and take up his cross, and follow Me . . . for what is a
man profited, if he shall gain the whole world, and lose his own
soul?" (KJV) Four campers presented different kinds of crosses
which we Christians try to carry.

The first speaker was a lovely young lady that everyone had
admired for her great personality and beauty. She came onto the
stage excitedly showing off a small gold cross that she wore
around her neck on a gold chain. It was beautiful indeed.

She then said, "Bob, you don't get the point. This is *my cross*, and it fits my personality with its beauty. It is the cross I have chosen for my life and I love it. I want to be popular and loved by everyone." She held it up again so everyone could admire it.

But Bob was not moved by her emotion and perspective on what was most important in this life and quietly asked if he could see the cross better. So she took it off and offered it to him. Bob responded, "This is beautiful indeed and so are you, but that is not what Christ meant when He said take up your cross. He has something much better for you and for the rest of us. A really beautiful life comes from giving your life to Christ Jesus and not from the selfishness that comes from the idea that being popular and lovely as the only thing to live for. I hope you realize that not everyone can have just what you described for we are not all so beautiful! You have to allow Christ to set your goals and actions."

The young lady was quite moved and bowed her head for a moment realizing she was only thinking of herself and did not have a goal that included a spiritual perspective. Then she did a remarkable thing. She took the cross from Bob's hands, laid it on the pulpit, and took her seat, trying not to show her feelings.

The next actor walked down the central aisle and carried a large cross about six inches wide and three feet tall. It was made out of quarter inch plywood and he had pasted all over the front a picture of a large castle-like home, a very expensive foreign car, a luxury yacht, and the other things that went with that lifestyle. Again, Bob pointed out that these things without Christ as the center of one's life come from only greed and the pride of life. It really had nothing to do with what Christ was talking about. Rather, it was based on the false concept that when wealth was the only thing in life it could become possessive and take over your whole personality until it destroys your life. It is a false view and understanding of what is really important.

Bob again referred to Jesus' words, and asked, "What will it profit a man to gain the whole world and lose his soul?" The actor hid his face in shame. Naturally, this idea of having things was important to the youth of Guatemala for most of them came from very poor families. There was a real hush in the room as the speaker broke his cross into pieces and threw it into the fireplace. He didn't say a word, nor did he have to, the kids were deeply moved.

The next actor was a seminary student who had been prominent in the activities of the camp and one of the cabin counselors. He had taken a couple of two by fours that were planed and polished to form a very lovely cross. It was sanded and waxed so that it really shone in the spotlight of the stage. He was careful to place it where it took advantage of the light and let the campers know that he really cherished it.

His words went with the beautiful cross, "I am about to

graduate from the seminary and my goal in life is to have the ability of Billy Graham. I have worked hard to make connections and am looking forward to having a large church, be on television and be the most popular speaker in Guatemala. Maybe someday I can move to the big country north of us and have all the prestige that goes with being the top man in our denomination."

"What a goal and perspective for your life," Bob commented. "I guess all of us would like to have that kind of position and prestige. But that certainly is not what Jesus was talking about. He did not think that the most important preacher was the most important one in the Kingdom of God. Do you really think that Jesus had that in mind when he talked about taking up your cross and following Him?"

For a moment, the actor seemed stunned, and gradually he took his polished cross over to the edge of the stage and laid it down and kissed it farewell. Everyone was quiet.

After a seemingly long pause, the favorite leader at the camp came from offstage to the left, into the light of the stage, struggling and stumbling with two huge branches of a small tree that had been nailed together to make a cross. The branch still had knots on it and several rough spots where others had been cut off. It was obviously very crude, heavy and uncomfortable. After the shock, the campers broke out in a loud laugh because he was obviously struggling with the heavy burden of his cross. The actor was very alert, and when they laughed, he took advantage of the moment and said in a loud voice, "It is so heavy and grinds into my shoulder. People laugh at me as I try to carry it around!"

He then turned to Bob and said, "Please help me get rid of this cross. It is too heavy and it hurts to carry it. I can't take it any longer. All I get is laughter or criticism for even trying. I want to throw it out and not have to carry it anymore."

All the campers where very still and you could hear a pin drop. What would Bob say to such a denial and startling declaration? He let the concept sink in for several minutes then quietly said to Fito, the actor, "Why don't you kneel down and give your burden to the Lord? He has a way to comfort the sore shoulder and relieve your burden. He did say, 'take up your cross and follow me.' Why don't you try kneeling down?" Slowly and deliberately, Fito knelt down, even though it was obviously a very painful action. A miracle happened as he knelt down, the crossbar of the cross rested on the floor and all the weight of the heavy burden was no longer there. It was gone. Fito looked up into the face of the crowd and smiled.

There was scarcely a dry eye in the room at the end of the service. It was obvious that everyone was thinking seriously of his relationship to Jesus Christ as we walked quietly down the short path to the campfire. When all had gathered at the Campfire Circle, a seminary student confessed that his ambition had been to be famous and to preach to huge crowds. As he threw his stick on the fire, he asked God to forgive him and then use him in any way He desired even if it meant a humble, small congregation. Others gave their testimonies as they placed their sticks on the fire speaking of how God had spoken to them about their idea of a cross and their misleading ideals and goals for life.

The flames had died down to just a few embers when Enrique came forward and asked for a stick. He was the young pastor who had been invited to be the speaker and Bible study leader at the youth conference. He and his wife had been facing a serious struggle but we had not been aware of it for he had given us some very challenging messages and did not seem concerned. This is the testimony that he shared with us as the fire died down.

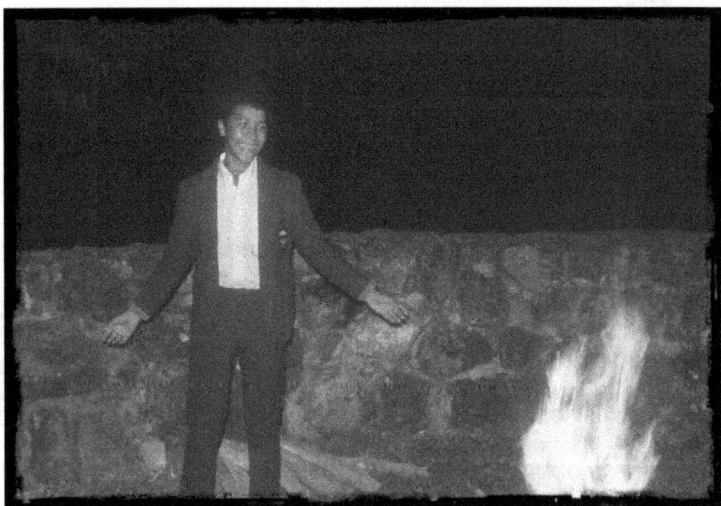

"My church, which is in a new barrio of Guatemala City, is very small and I and my wife have a new baby to support and feed. Since the church is so small they can hardly pay me much of a salary and there are not enough givers to rent a manse. As a temporary solution, I and my wife have been living in one of the bedrooms of the home of one of the elders, sharing their kitchen and one bath. This has grown into a crisis since the finances of the church have not improved and the small home is really not adequate to accommodate our two families. It has been six months now and both the elder and I feel that to avoid friction it is time for a change to be made. My wife and I are looking for some kind of solution and hoping that here at camp we can decide what God wants us to do. I have a teaching degree so maybe I should give up the ministry."

With tears in his eyes, he told us that before his conversion he was involved with the communist party trying to overthrow the government. After his conversion, he felt led to go into the ministry and use his talents for the Lord. Now, because of his poverty and living conditions, he and his wife had decided to give up the ministry. It was too much of a sacrifice — he had no place for his family to live, not enough income to pay their bills and a family to feed. They had discussed it and decided that the struggles and the sacrifices of the ministry were too great and they could no longer take it. They had been looking for another job where they could have some of the things they had dreamed of when they were married.

Then he said, "I am ashamed tonight. I have been reminded of what Christ expects of us, His followers, and I don't care what it costs, I just want to spend my life serving Him." Symbolically he knelt down to indicate that the crossbar of the cross was to rest on the ground. "I now see that the Lord could and will help us." All the campers were deeply moved and were ready to give their lives to Jesus knowing that He would lift the weight of the cross from their shoulders too.

A few years later Esther and I visited the church where Enrique was pastor, and God was in the process of working another miracle. God had honored his faithfulness. The church had grown and they were able to purchase two lots, one on each side of the old building, and the members were in the process of constructing a larger sanctuary because there was no room for everyone in the original building. One of the lots had a manse, so Enrique and his family had their own home with a nice patio and didn't have to live in the back room of one of the elders' homes. The new home was made of adobe bricks but later they would build a more suitable home. His salary was not excessive but it was adequate for their needs, and they were so happy because God had responded to their decision to "take up your cross daily and follow Me" (Luke 9:23, KJV).

Don Yo-Yo
Monte Sión, Guatemala, 1958

The group was a select one, and rather small in size. These young people were the leaders from the twenty-five Christian Endeavor Societies of the Presbyterian Churches of the Synod of Guatemala. They were the cream of the crop in more ways than one. They had come to Monte Sión for a special retreat to be trained to develop better programs and leaders for the individual youth societies. They enjoyed their time together as they shared and talked about how to better live the Christian life and how they could lead the youth under their care into a deeper and more meaningful life style that would honor Jesus Christ.

The program for the retreat featured don Yo-Yo, or as it was translated, *Mr. Ego*. The campers got to know don Yo-Yo the first day. He was introduced by illustrated comic posters showing the life style of don Yo-Yo. You know how a yo-yo runs up and down its own string. It goes down seemingly to do something and then gets cold feet and runs back up into the player's hand again. A yo-yo never seems to get

MR. YO-YO

anywhere but is only involved with itself with no thought of others! Since the program was at Monte Sión camp among Spanish speaking campers, it was easy to make a play on words. In Spanish the word for *I* is *Yo,* so don Yo-Yo is a person who is only involved in *I* or self. He only thinks of himself, is very selfish and self-centered. The whole program was built around what to do about this philosophy of only satisfying self and never thinking of others. If one is not careful, his life becomes fully self-centered and all his thinking and actions are interested only in his own little world. The consequences result in hurting others, insults, and a discourteous, hurtful life style. A good leader of youth has to learn this principle. There were several posters that illustrated the conceited life of don Yo-Yo: It seems that he knows nothing of love, compassion, kindness and concern for others.

After a couple of days, we invited Dr. Mario Rios, director of the hospital in Guatemala City to visit us at camp to share how this lifestyle affected our personal relationship with people of the other gender. He asked, "Are you the selfish, inconsiderate, one who hurts and destroys others' lives by what you say, and above all, by what you do?" Later that evening we asked Dr. Rios to check up on don Yo-Yo, for he had become quite ill during the days at the Retreat. After the supposed exam, he announced to the campers that the patient was getting worse, no doubt because of the changes taking place in the thinking of the campers. He told us that it would be better to take don Yo-Yo back to town and put him in the hospital.

The next day a telegram came from Dr. Rios, "Come and get the remains of don Yo-Yo because he passed away in the night." We went to the little town of Amatitlán and bought a child's coffin in the marketplace. The coffin was about two feet long and made out of plain pine boards. We cut out a small area in the lid so the campers could look in at the remains before the coffin was carried away for the burial service. As the campers filed past the coffin and looked inside to see the remains, they looked into a mirror. *Self* had died there at camp.

After a good discussion of the life of a leader, we encouraged the campers to hold a funeral service for don Yo-Yo in the chapel and then have a procession carrying the coffin down to a spot near the campfire circle where they had chosen to bury him. The circle had a warm fire burning and each one was encouraged to think about his life and the way he represented Christ to the youth of Guatemala. The question was asked, "How well do you live by God's principles?"

Because don Yo-Yo was so egotistical he couldn't live in that Christian atmosphere and the lesson was to see to it that he departed from the personality of each camper there at camp. His burial spot is still marked with a tombstone, which is right along the path to the campfire area, where everyone will see it. The cross above the grave is a timely reminder that when *self* is

crucified and buried with Christ, one has a "New life in Christ."
Don Yo-Yo has become a byword among the leaders of our
church and one often hears the comment, "Well, don Yo-Yo, I
thought you were buried at Monte Sión."

LIFE ON THE FIELD

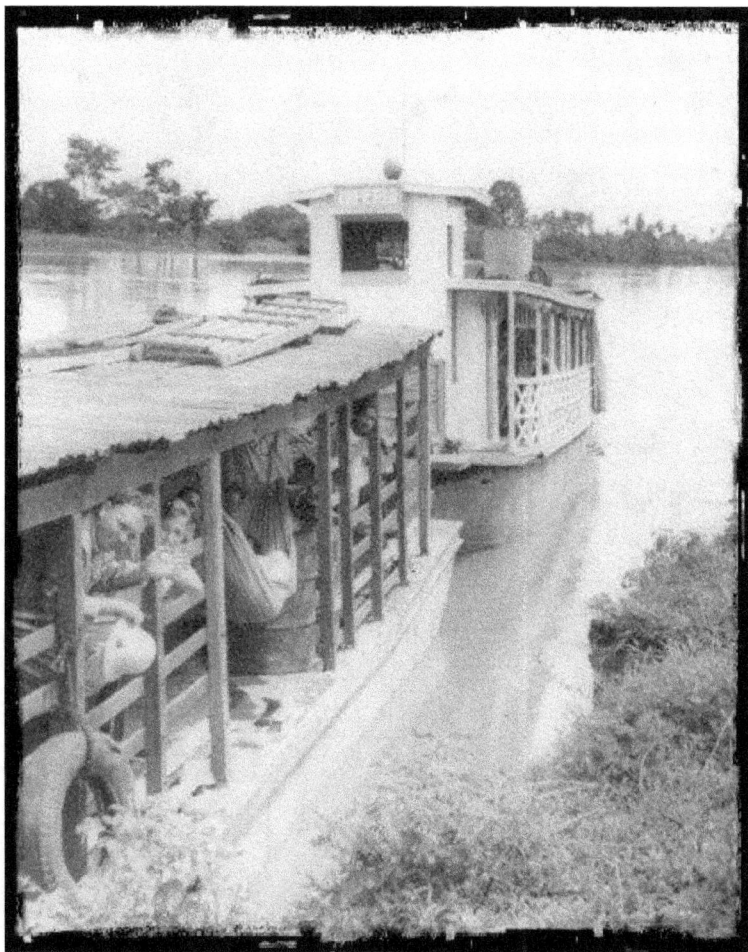

Adjusting to the Mission Field
Columbia, 1946

To get to the mission field in Colombia, South America, we began by taking the train from Los Angeles. Our first stop was Fort Worth, Texas, where we spent all of one day sitting on the siding waiting to be connected to the train to Brownsville, Texas. We spent the night in a hotel in Brownsville. The next day we boarded a DC 3 airplane on the first leg of our flight to Colombia. The plane had only 21 seats and since we had never traveled by plane before, we found that experienced travelers had taken all the double seats and we couldn't sit together. I was bothered a bit because I needed John to hold my hand on that plane! Our first stop was Mexico City. It was a long stop and we were asked to get off the plane and wait in the airport while they refueled the plane. The next leg took us to Guatemala City, where we arrived late in the afternoon. We spent the night in the old Palace Hotel. We were quite impressed with its old world classic style. That evening we walked up and down the block but didn't dare wander around to other streets for fear of getting lost. Everyone spoke Spanish and we didn't! Before daylight, we were awakened, very early, by the bells of the Catholic Church next door and commented how different life would be in Latin America.

Soon we were back at the airport and boarded our plane for Panama. The flight stopped in El Salvador, Nicaragua, Costa Rica and when we got near Panama, the steward pulled down the shades so we would not be able to see the Panama Canal. Since World War II was just over, there was fear that someone would bomb the canal and they did not want anyone on the plane to have a way to pinpoint the locks where sabotage could be done. We had to spend two days in Panama City waiting for space on the flight to Medellín, Colombia. Our first impression of Panama City was that the black maids in the hotel spoke Spanish with a southern accent. We did walk around with more confidence and got a hint of what life would be like as new missionaries. We were so impressed by the slums and poverty and were disheartened by these conditions. We did not understand a word they said and wondered how long it would be before we could really be missionaries.

Upon arrival at the airport in Medellín, Colombia we were met by Allan Schotmot who was a welcome sight in this strange land. We had met Allan and his wife in New York at the outgoing missionary conference. He had already studied one semester at the language school and was able to converse with the customs officials and help us find a taxi to get to our new home.

May 1946
Medellín, Columbia

Dearest Mother and Daddy,

We are living in a typical Colombian home where all the rooms open onto an open patio. Lee and Eleanor Stewart and baby Jeannie have the front room on one side of the entrance corridor and Señorita Rizo, a teacher at the school, lives in the room on the other side. Next to her room is the dining room which has become a classroom since Miss Rizo challenges us to ask for things in Spanish. It is fun, but does get frustrating when you can't think of the Spanish word for salt or bread. After unpacking our suitcases we walked over to the large home that serves as our school. The LaPorts are very kind but very strict, and expect us to dig right in for 6 hours a day. In the afternoons, we walk downtown and try to speak to the market folks to practice our newly learned Spanish vocabulary. The merchants are very patient and help us pronounce our new words correctly. Since every house has a maid to do the cooking, we don't have home duties and are soon involved in this foreign language of the home and everyday life.

Nov. 12, 1946

You may wonder why I am writing with the typewriter. It's easier to type than write when one is only half sitting up in bed. Last Monday evening our expected child threatened to cause some trouble. I had started bleeding and was very worried. We had waited several years for our first child. I went right to bed while Johnny went to get the mission nurse who came at once. I didn't dare turn over all night long. Nothing more has happened. I had shots all week and when the doctor came on Thursday, he chided me for being so lazy and finding an excuse to take life so easy. Vera, our missionary nurse has come every day to rub my back and braid my hair. Everything seems to be back to normal now and I didn't lose the baby!

Johnny has been wonderful through it all. He stayed home from school the first two days to look after me. I suppose the maid could have taken care of me, but my Spanish is so limited it was very comforting to have him here. There is a group of Mennonites in our school and they came, sang, read Scripture and prayed for me. One of them said something I will never forget, "The Lord sometimes sends things that we can't understand. *It's easier to look up when we are lying on our backs.*"

A month or so later:

We have just put in another eventful week! Mr. Shaul, one of the Presbyterian missionaries from Barranquilla was just here to visit with us and told us we were urgently needed in the Sinú Valley where we probably will be assigned. He told us, "Because there are no missionaries there at all now, I and a national worker went up to visit the churches, have meetings and give them encouragement. One town we stopped in we found a large number of people who wanted to worship, so we got them together in a rented building. There has never been a church there. After a week, we organized a church with over 100 members and a communicants class. There is an average attendance of 200 a night and we left them as an organized church going in full swing."

It seems a miracle to us, but in reality, work has been going on in that area for a long time. Dick Baird had established an evangelical community nearby on the mission farm. Mr. Shaul just happened to be there when it was time to organize them into a church. "This is only a sample of the whole River Sinú area," he told us. There are little villages all along the river with the need of a missionary. But one can hardly visit them except by river boat which goes only once a week. The trip Dick Shaul made took three days by boat. They had nothing but cookies to eat, because one doesn't dare eat or drink what they serve or most likely would never come out alive. Here every bit of water we drink has to be boiled or else we will come down with any number of tropical diseases. On such a trip, one has to drink warm cokes for the entire trip or else do without. That is where we are probably going to be assigned!

Using the road is out of the question for about six months of the year because the heavy rains flood the areas between the towns. We will discuss this assignment and the transportation needs at the mission meeting in December which will meet in Barranquilla.

Dec. 1946

After nine months at language school, we moved to Barranquilla, a port city on the hot coast, to attend the Mission Meeting and were assigned to the Sinú Valley. Dr. Richard Shaul, from that station, was anxious to have us move at once to replace the Emersons who had been forced to leave the missionary home in Cereté, which is about an hour's ride in a dugout canoe from the main town of Montería. The home is right on the river, a simple missionary residence that is fully screened for protection from the malaria mosquitoes. That is our destination as soon as our child is born. After listening to all that discussion and concern it came to me that we must look for God's will. He has it all worked out so what is the use of worrying about it. (Margaret Lynn "Peggy" arrived April 1, 1947)

Feb. 14, 1948
Montería, Colombia

The Mission did not force us to go to Cereté. It is not central, and the church there has a pastor who is capable of directing the ministry. We have gone to the capital of the department which is Montería. It is more in the center of things and makes it easier for John to catch the boat to travel up river where most of the churches are.

We are so glad to get here at last. It is very hot with only a slight breeze. But I would really as soon stand the heat as the *wind* that we had in Barranquilla. It banged the doors and windows, it blew hair in your face, it flopped clothes so that you could scarcely hang them up, and worst of all, it blew dust into the house so that an hour after you cleaned, everything was gritty again. I suppose that after a few months of such heat I will be wishing for some *brisa* again. On Wednesday evening, we packed the truck, that is John, Dick, Bill Miller and two Colombian fellows did. The truck is army surplus bought from Panama after the war. I stayed up to pack their lunch and do some last minute packing and ironing for Milly. (Milly is the nurse that will live with us till the clinic is built in Nazarét and Mrs. Libreros is the pastor's wife who is going to live in Nazarét).

John, Milly and Señora Libreros left at 1:30 a.m. It is about an 18 hour trip and John preferred to do the first part at night as travel is cooler. Most of the trip is hot and the dirt roads are full of pot holes. I left on the plane 6 a.m. on Friday. Peggy was as good as gold and didn't get sick. John and Milly met me when the plane landed in Montería at 9:30. We came right to the hotel.

It was rather warm in the afternoon and Peggy didn't sleep much and was a bit fussy. John brought the truckload of stuff from Cereté and we set up Peggy's bed so she has been able to sleep better. I brought a lot of boiled water from Barranquilla, enough to last until this afternoon. She has been eating out of cans as usual. That isn't okay because I have to give her all of one thing and I cannot make any cereal. She has decided she doesn't like Pablum! In a few days, I hope we get used to the hotel. They knock on your door at 5 a.m. to serve you a little cup of *tinto*, a very sweet hot coffee. Neither John nor I like it so wish they would skip us and let us sleep a bit more. But it gets so hot so very early that I guess the folks start the day early when it is more pleasant.

Now comes the most wonderful part. When we arrived, we didn't know where we were going to live. The hotel will be okay for a few days, but with no way to boil water and having to eat their native food it is hard with Peggy. Now we found this lovely rented apartment. It isn't even finished yet so is nice and clean. No lights or water. We have been able to store our things there, however. It is large enough for us and Milly. Living room, dining room, pantry, kitchen and three rooms up front, one for our bedroom, one for a study and one for Peggy. There is a separate room with bath for Milly. I am so glad that it is on the second floor. John is away quite a bit of the time so we will be safer that way. We have a few problems, such as no living room furniture, no stove or water filter, but we will get those things straightened out. We can hardly wait to move in.

March 8, 1948

We are in the apartment but I have been a bit tired and discouraged. We have had all our meals late and were up late at night doing dishes. But things have let up now and we are settled in. We have had no water for days. John had to install a suction pump to draw water out of the main water pipe. The water comes only for a couple of hours daily and the folks downstairs just leave their faucets on all the time so when the water does come they will fill their tanks. There is no pressure to get it up to us since we are on the second floor. We have had to buy water from a boy who brought it from the river on a donkey and charged us 25 centavos a gallon delivered to the kitchen. With the pump, we have our own water but have to boil it. Now we at least have water in our faucets and it is clean.

Montería is not a large town but does have some canned food in the stores. Everything is so expensive, though no more than Barranquilla. There just aren't any green things in the market place. The only thing is cabbage and a few tough green beans. No wonder we have to live out of cans. Milly has a small pressure cooker which is what we need for the meat. We can get tomatoes, platano, yucca and potatoes. Milk comes fresh from the cows that are marched down the street and the herdsman milks it directly into your container. He goes by the house and rings a little bell to let you know he and the cow have come. Milly bought a small kerosene stove with an oven but it is a bit hard to regulate, still it helps with the cooking problems. We have made some pies, cookies and an upside down cake that was soggy and tough.

August 12, 1948
Mission Meeting in Bogotá

This is our second Mission Meeting. Bogotá is about 8,000 feet altitude and cold after living in Montería. We had a vacation coming so went to the Mission rest home in Santa Ana, near Bogotá, for a few days. The place used to be a railroad camp. There are three houses, one for the caretaker and a big recreation hall. There are orange and grapefruit trees and pineapple plants. It's on a hill and you look out over valleys and rolling mountains. You can see it is a lovely restful place. I wasn't feeling very well on Friday, diarrhea and tummy ache. On Saturday afternoon, I was rolling around on the bed with cramps. We didn't want to take any chance on appendicitis so we got a taxi and came back to Bogatá and the doctor. He said it was only the Bogotá Blitz and gave me some medicine and the next day I was better but spent two days in bed. Since they found that Daddy had glaucoma and you warned me about having a checkup, we also went to see an ophthalmologist. No one could recommend a good one in Barranquilla and in Montería there are none so I got a name from the doctor in Bogotá. This doctor says that I have glaucoma too! The left eye isn't bad, the field of vision scarcely damaged at all and the pressure is only a little high, but the right eye must be watched carefully. The left part of the field of vision has closed in somewhat and the pressure is about 21, so I must be checked every 15 days and must think of the possibility of surgery on that eye.

So, what to do? I'm writing to Dr. Clothier right away as he is the head of medical work at the New York headquarters. The medical committee of the mission will send recommendations to him also. No one in Montería can do the necessary checkups so Barranquilla is the nearest place. There is the possibility of living either here in Bogotá or there for a couple of months but I don't want to be away from John so long, even though he will be in Nazarét a good deal of the time building the clinic. He should have a place to come back to and he can't go to where the nurses are even though there are two of them. There is the other possibility of going to the States right away, but there is the same objection of John's being alone. We may have to antedate our furlough (due after July 1st). The clinic he is building will be done by the end of the year. John will be worn out if not sick by that time, he always comes home with something like malaria or worse after a week or so in the upper Sinú . . .

End of August 1948

After much prayer and thought, we have changed our minds — or at least I have. John was always pretty much of that mind. We feel now that I should go back to the States right away. As Martha Emerson, our predecessor in the Sinú, says, "If I were to stay here and anything were to go wrong I would always be sorry, but if I go to the States and anything goes wrong I will know that I have done the best I could." All of the medical people of the Mission feel the same way and Dr. Clothier of the Mission Board feels that I should come home at once. I will let you know when I get some answers. I still have to leave John but he wants me to go, so I will. There is the question of where I'd stay, and as far as I am concerned, it would preferably be with you, if you have room. John's folks have room, I know, but it would be hard on Mom Shackelford because of her cancer. Pray that we do the right thing.

Ever so much love, Esther

Esther and Peggy flew home to Pasadena within the month via Jamaica and Miami. Surgery on her eye was done immediately and she stayed with her mother and daddy until John was permitted to come home in July 1949, for "home assignment."

What He Feeds Me I Will Swallow
Colombia, South America, 1947

Our work often took us to small villages along the Sinú
River in the jungles of Northwest Colombia. It is an area that is
very primitive and wild and we were dependent on the natives for
food and places to stay. Tierralta was a village only a few miles
from the Panamanian border. There were several believers in the
village and now and then we would have a special week of
meetings that were well attended. Mark Mathews, a native pastor
who had gone to our Bible school and was pastor of the
Presbyterian Church in Cartagena, joined me one week for
evangelistic meetings. He did most of the preaching since I was
fresh out of language school. The attendance was good. I
remember that there was a prostitute coming to the meetings
whom the congregation had been praying for to make a
commitment to Christ and become a part of their fellowship. One
night there was great rejoicing when she accepted the Lord. Soon
they wanted to have their own church and requested the Mission
to help buy a lot where they could put up a building. Later I was
assigned to supervise the construction of that building and lived
with them in the village for several weeks at a time.

We often stayed in the home of an elder who had built a
humble hut for his family out of straw, corn stalks, and bamboo.

A mud plaster over the bamboo gave them some privacy. Of course, there was an outhouse at the back of the lot. He had a small plot where he could raise some corn and keep a few chickens that were allowed to run free. The father had rented property nearby where he raised the yearly crop of rice. We had to sleep in hammocks that were stretched out anywhere there was room, usually in the outer corridor of the home. They were so glad to have visitors to lead them in worship that they always fed us the best they had.

Their diet consisted mostly of rice, which was the main crop of the Sinú Valley and they had three or four ways to serve it. Coco palms were in abundance, so the most popular dish was *arroz con coco*. Another interesting dish was made of boiled yucca, a cassava root. It grew in almost every back yard – with papaya, bananas and coconuts - and was served regularly as a side dish. Of course, the high starch content was not good for my diet, but it was delicious the way they cooked it. It was boiled and served hot like potatoes and heavily flavored with pig grease. One day, as we were sitting under the palm roof of their dirt-floor outdoor lean-to that served as a dining area, I found that the food was even less appetizing than usual and a bit difficult to swallow. I soon began to look for a way to skip that meal. We always took care not to insult them and did not refuse to eat, no matter what they offered us. They had often gone without, just to give us their best, so I could not refuse to eat what was put before me, even that day. I quietly said this prayer, "Where He leads me I will follow, and what He feeds me I will swallow," and then gingerly

started to eat.

But I just had to do something about that food. So when I noticed there were pigs and chickens along with dogs hanging around the table hoping we would accidentally drop a little morsel, I decided that might be a good solution to the unsavory dish. I could accommodate the animals and, maybe, also save face. I tried to slip the worst part of my food off the plate and let it drop to the ground when no one was looking. That would let the animals have something to eat and still hide my sins. What a mistake! No sooner did it fall to the ground than the emaciated dogs, pigs and chickens make a mad dash to fight over it, even before it hit the ground. The family never ate with their guests, but they stood around watching and the children were always looking through the cracks in the bamboo walls of the kitchen hut. The minute I dropped something it was obvious to everyone what I had done and the whole family stared at me as if to say, "Don't you like what we serve you?" I felt so guilty and I was

sure they all were thinking, here we have given our best to feed the *gringo* and he doesn't even appreciate it!

The food was not the only challenge about staying in Tierralta. No one had a shower or bathtub. The men invited the male visitors to simply go down to the river to bathe in the nude. There was a huge mango tree along the path to the river and I noticed that the men would often pick a mango and peel it and take bites as they walked along. By the time they reached the river it was all eaten except the huge seed and skins which they threw into the river. The river was bordered by heavy tropical trees and a clearing was maintained where the horses and riders could cross over. This was the favorite bathing spot. During the day the women would come down and wash their clothes on the rocks and then take a sponge bath along with their washing. I commented on the fact that the children never went swimming and asked why. "It is too dangerous," they said, "There are snakes in the vines that even swim in the water and there are fish in the river that bite."

When they said, "fish in the river," my interest was sparked, and I asked if they ever went fishing. The answer was that they had no fish hooks and had never tried. So, on my next trip home to Barranquilla, I bought some fish hooks and some line to try out that most likely fishing hole. Sure enough, it worked. I made a bamboo pole, tied the line to the end of it, and used the mango as bait. It was just as I had suspected, the ripe mango had become a favorite fish food. I dropped the line into the ripples where the river changed course and, bingo, a nice big fish immediately took the bait - hook, line and sinker. It was a large one; I could tell by the way it took the hook. But alas, the men were right, it had teeth and many of them. In a moment it had cut the line and was gone hook and all. It simply bit through the line.

There were no fishing supplies at the small store in town because they only sold the bare necessities like sugar, salt, *panela* for sugar and a few cans of sardines. So I could not buy any kind of steel leader for the fish hooks to keep the fish from biting through the line. I talked to the workmen about the problem. None of them had heard of such a thing as piano wire or any similar thing, but they were very interested in why the "big one got away." They would do anything to help for they were excited about adding fish to their diet of *arroz con coco*. But none of them could come up with a solution of any kind. I knew strong twine wouldn't work and I needed a leader of a tiny piece of wire. No such thing seemed to exist in that faraway place. We finally settled on taking a piece of baling wire about a foot long and tying it to the end of the line and bending it to hold the fishhook.

Just about everyone in town was in on the project by then and they all came to watch me fish at the bathing hole along the river. I put a piece of mango on the hook and dropped it into the river in the exact spot where the men threw their mango seeds and peelings. I didn't have to wait. The minute the bait hit the water there was a flash and I had one on the line! Slowly I worked it to shore. The men were right, it was large and had a lot of sharp teeth. No wonder they didn't want to swim in the river. It must have weighed over a couple of pounds. What a change in diet that made; now we all had *arroz con pescado*. I put on another piece of mango and tried again but didn't catch another fish that day. I tried all the things my father had taught me about fishing in the ocean at Newport Beach but there was not another bite. I guess all the commotion and loss of their grandfather fish had scared the rest of them away.

The next day the pastor suggested that he would like to try

and could he use my pole and hook? Apparently, the joy of eating fish when they had only had rice pleased him and the whole family. Of course, I encouraged him to try. And he was as successful as I had been! One fish, but no more than one that day. All the fish were either wary or had fled. The fish would not bite again. But every day they were able to catch at least one. I discovered that the old saying was true, "teach a man to fish and he will feed himself." Tierralta had discovered a new industry.

Cost of Discipleship
Jungles of Colombia, 1947

Luke 14:25-33 says, "And there went great multitudes with him: and he turned, and said unto them, If any man come to me, and hate not his father, and mother, and wife, and children, and brethren, and sisters, yea, and his own life also, he cannot be my disciple. And whosoever doth not bear his cross, and come after me, cannot be my disciple. For which of you, intending to build a tower, sitteth not down first, and counteth the cost, whether he have sufficient to finish it? Lest haply, after he hath laid the foundation, and is not able to finish it, all that behold it begin to mock him, Saying, This man began to build, and was not able to finish. Or what king, going to make war against another king, sitteth not down first, and consulteth whether he be able with ten thousand to meet him that cometh against him with twenty thousand? Or else, while the other is yet a great way off, he sendeth an ambassage, and desireth conditions of peace. So likewise, whosoever he be of you that forsaketh not all that he hath, he cannot be my disciple."

David R. Befus, president of the Latin American Mission, sums up the missionary life this way: "They are confronted with a call to a mission that involves sacrifice and risk. They leave the peaceful, secure context of their homeland to take on a cause greater than themselves. They face hardship, loneliness, a new cultural context, strange languages and a variety of people unlike themselves. They also confront evil because they present the good news directly against the powers of darkness and against spiritual forces of evil." (Eph. 6:12). We didn't think along these lines but simply went because we felt God was calling us to take the gospel to others. We did give up just about everything to go to Colombia, South America. But it was a blessing to see the fulfillment that God gave in our lives and ministry. We no longer could be with our families, it is true, for we now lived in a strange culture, and dearly missed our friends and relationships. It was quite a move to go into an uncertain life in a strange land that spoke a strange language.

After nine months of language school at Medellín, we were assigned to work and live in the Sinú Valley with the *campesinos* of the jungles near the Panamanian border. The towns of Cereté and Montería were the jumping off place for the three day river boat trip into this primitive area. The mission had established a center and home for missionaries in the small town of Cereté. Temporarily, Esther lived in the city of Barranquilla with two other missionary families until Peggy was born. I traveled back and forth by air, boat, mule back and the local bus to the pueblos of the Sinú Valley. Have you ever traveled for eight hours on a bus that only stops in small towns where there are no public bathrooms? The bus had no glass in the windows due to the intense heat and humidity. Thus, the passengers could catch any bit of breeze that came along while hoping that it would not rain. The bus was called a *chivo,* or goat, because of its ability to go anywhere, road or no road. Former missionaries had established several family gatherings at their ranchos and I was to visit and encourage as many of them as possible. The larger town of Nazarét was the only place with a pastor. The small villages had house church meetings wherever there were believers, led by the father or a neighbor.

Homes were usually made of grass or bamboo, sometimes plastered with mud. They were huts with a hot tin roof and a lean-to extension added at the back that served as a living room, kitchen and dining room. The cooking area consisted of an elevated platform with a bed of sand that held the cooking fire. This is where the wife prepared the meals, cooked in clay pots or on lids from 50-gallon drums placed over the coals which were perfect for warming tortillas or frying. The fuel was charcoal that the home owner had prepared himself by partially burning green wood stacked and covered with mud. This lean-to kitchen was large enough to hold a small pine table and over this, I was allowed to hang up my hammock for the night. This gave me protection from the rain since it was under a grass or tin roof and most nights I was able to get a fairly good night's sleep. The floor was dirt, but sprinkled with water daily, and swept to keep it clean and dust free. Under the circumstances, it was not that bad.

Because of the heat, I left my suitcase at home. By wrapping a sheet, a toothbrush, a razor and a couple of T-shirts in the folds of the hammock, there was no need of a bulky suitcase. I washed out my underwear and T-shirt each evening before going to bed. Being in the tropics things quickly dried out, ready for wearing the next day. I had a very special *toldo*, which was a mosquito net with sleeves at the end so it would go over the ropes at the ends of the hammock and hang down all the way to the ground. This was supposed to keep the mosquitoes out of my sleeping area. Experienced natives taught me how to sleep at an angle in the native hammock so it would give me an almost level sleeping area and it worked pretty well.I was able to visit most of the preaching points during the month or six weeks that I spent with them. The travel was by riverboat and donkey, but I soon found a way to buy a motorcycle that would get me from one preaching point to another in a few hours instead of days and so avoid getting sore from the saddle.

After about six weeks of this life, I was able to get back home to Barranquilla and spend a few days with the family. While in the big city, I had to visit the doctor and replenish my medicine, Atabrine, which I had to take to protect me from malaria. Malaria was very prevalent and the mosquitoes got under the toldo now and then. They actually bit me many times and I ended up with five malaria attacks during the three years of our term of service. By the time we went home on furlough I had taken so much Atabrine that I was turning yellow and was not aware that I had yellow jaundice from those primitive living conditions. That is a good name for hepatitis, for one really turns yellow and it leaves one very depleted.

After a week or so at home in Barranquilla, it was back to the jungles of the Sinú Valley for another visit to the congregations and a time to encourage the folks in the Lord. It was a great joy to see many come to know Jesus as Lord and Savior. It was a good time and very fulfilling watching God at work in this neglected and primitive area.

When we accepted our appointment to Colombia, South America, we were advised to buy good beds in the States to take with us. We took other basic things with us also. I just had to have a portable typewriter, small library of sermons, theological books and some favorite wrenches. These we kept in packing boxes until we could have a permanent home. It was good for us to live out of boxes while with the other two families because it was truly a learning experience which taught us a deeply committed life. The Lord knew we still had to learn to depend more on Him and not to think we could manage on our own. One tends to think that his training, wits, and personal abilities are all that are needed.

We were asked to store most of our worldly goods at the empty mission house in the town of Cereté which was the center of the work and located on the Sinú River. We were expected to make it our home after Peggy arrived, so everything was shipped from the big city of Barranquilla even though we would not be able to move there for several months. I hired a believer to sleep in the house and keep the thieves away. It was easy to find a watchman since the elders in the church recommended a member who was out of work and willing to look after our things. They assured me that he was honest and faithful. He was ready to move in that same day. He slept in a back room and fixed his meals on the back porch and took over the house while I was away visiting the churches. The house was a typical tropical building with a tin roof. It had six rooms and a bath, with a corridor along the front to connect the rooms. In the back was a boarded up room for storage. The house was fully screened to protect us from the mosquitoes and to catch any breeze that came along in that jungle heat. This screening was very important but made the house vulnerable when no one was there. Would you believe it, the Lord even took away most of those few things we had brought from the States and cherished so much? After locking almost all of our worldly goods in the one back room that was enclosed as a store room, I again went up river to visit the believers preaching and teaching in their home churches.

After making my regular visit, I returned to Barranquilla and home. This large city was about three or four days distance by public transportation from home so I often took the DC-3 airplane from Montería that got me there in about three hours. Sometimes Esther and I would spend our vacations at the mission vacation house at the beach.

On my next visit to Cereté, I was greeted by the leading elder of the church with the sad story that a thief had broken into the house and taken almost everything. The watchman who was recommended for his faithfulness had fled and no one seemed to know where he was. It was a very sad report that I took back to Esther when I returned home to Barranquilla. But we had to learn this lesson well and the Lord knew that my ego and self-assurance still needed to be dealt with.

One trip I went on horseback to visit the churches and to preach and teach the folks in Sienaga Grande and in the small village of Salamina, which is way off the beaten track. It had a simple store with a single table and some shelves to display the inventory of things that were bought by the people of the small village. It was the front room of one of the huts and it only sold what they called bare necessities such as kerosene, rice, salt, beans and sugar. They had an abundance of panela, a cake made of sugarcane which they made themselves. Sometimes there would be a couple of cans of sardines on the shelves. They would let me sleep on the counter when I visited that village which I appreciated as it was off the dirt floor and fairly clean.

It was in this village that I had an experience that changed my whole life. The service went on until almost midnight, but they would not go home because the occasion was so special for them. It meant getting together as Christians, which was rare and a real community event. There was no entertainment in that area. Life consisted of long days of work in the hot sun and at nightfall, they gathered around the coals of the cooking area to visit. To keep the mosquitoes away they threw green branches and leaves on the coals so that the smoke would keep them away, but it was not very pleasant. When a visitor came they wanted to sit up all night to sing, talk, hear from the Bible and visit. So after I ran out of anything more to say, the service ended and we just sat around and enjoyed the Christian fellowship. About midnight, most began to drift away to their homes, but a couple of young men stayed behind to ask me to come and visit their village. They told me that they lived about eight kilometers away through the jungle and had never had anyone come to hold a service in their home. But I just couldn't accept and go with them because of promises made to visit other places the next day. That night I watched them walk off into the jungles and I am afraid there were tears in my eyes as that tiny kerosene lantern disappeared into the night. They didn't have money for flashlight batteries nor could they even buy any in that isolated area. These men pleaded with me to go with them. They said they would spend the night and wait for me if I would only visit their small village the next day. They too wanted to gather their friends and neighbors to study the Word, sing and have a time of fellowship. Each of these villages consisted of more or less 20 adults and their children. Three or four families lived close together and formed a center. They were Christians and wanted to hear about Jesus too. I doubt if a missionary has ever been able to visit them and share the gospel there. It was one of the hardest decisions of my life to say no. I have never been able to forget having to say *no* to them.

The Lord knew I had to go through this. It was another necessary humbling because I thought that being a college graduate and having seminary training made me superior to all of those country peasants. In fact, their love for Christ and faithfulness was far superior to mine. God just had to teach me that my ego needed a little mending. Actually, no one person had the time to visit everywhere but I had thought I could. A missionary in that setting gets to feel quite superior and thinks he is able to win the whole world all by himself. But God didn't really bless me in His work there until I realized that He could and would do His work very well without me unless I had a better attitude. I soon realized that one is effective only when he is a tool in the hands of the Holy Spirit and lets God take the leadership of his life and lets Him work through his attitude.

I like what E. Stanley Jones says about this, "Man has shown an infinite ability to trip over himself and to sprawl in the dust of humiliation when he elevates himself to a tin god." I soon discovered that when you want a miracle you had better let God do it. "Dear God, when I strut I stumble. When I surrender, then I succeed. Dear Lord, let me stumble once in a while."

Dwight and John Drive to Guatemala
Mexico, 1950

In 1950, the Mission Board assigned us to Guatemala. This was a transfer from Colombia because of Esther's medical condition. During our term in Colombia, the doctor found that she had glaucoma and they felt that we would be better off in Guatemala than the Sinú Valley of Colombia because there was a doctor there who was a diplomate of the Ophthalmology Association of America. The Lord was good to us and this was a great relief since the director of the Latin American Division of the Presbyterian Mission Board had bluntly recommended that we seek a pastorate in the USA after finding she had this disease. We did not want to give up being missionaries so we had taken our problem to the doctor in Pasadena who had treated Esther's father for the same disease. Being a Christian and great promoter of missions, he was anxious to find a way for us to fulfill the mission board's requirements and help us continue our career as missionaries. Upon our visit for a checkup, he took the time to look up the Association membership and found that Dr. Quevedo of Guatemala was a member. Upon reporting this to the mission board, they enthusiastically responded and soon we were assigned to go to Guatemala.

At the end of World War II, it was difficult to buy cars since none had been manufactured for the public during the years of the war. Fortunately, we had been able to buy a car by going to the dealer in Barranquilla, Colombia before leaving on furlough. The dealer there told us that there were no cars available in the USA because of the long waiting lists on the dealer's desks after the war. Many were anxious to obtain a new car because all the second hand ones had been bought up during the war years. The Colombia dealer told me that he had a new Oldsmobile available but it was still in the showrooms of New York. Since the first stop on my way home from Colombia was a visit to the mission board offices in New York, I purchased the car right on the spot for cash. Everyone in Colombia wanted US dollars and he was glad to sell to me because that's what I had. We took delivery in New York after talking to the mission board and had a new Olds to drive to California.

Esther had gone home nine months earlier to have surgery on her eyes and she took the train from California to New York to meet me there. What a reunion that was after nine months of separation. The next day we reported to the board to discuss our future with the director of the Latin America field.

When we were assigned to Guatemala we were told that the Oldsmobile would not be a good car for those poor roads and were directed to buy another car. We were able to trade it for a Chevy station wagon that was quite acceptable to the missionaries in Guatemala. Esther was expecting Freddy and so it was recommended that she and Peggy, now three, fly instead of going with me in the new station wagon. Dwight Goodenough offered to help me drive through Mexico to Guatemala. Dwight and LaRue had been great supporters of our ministry on the mission field since the beginning and their church was one of our major supporters. It was a great answer to prayer to have him offer to help me for it would have been impossible to make that 11-day trip alone.

From one of Esther's letters home, sent after we arrived in Guatemala:

"For John and Dwight, in the station wagon, it was a personal acquaintance with every chuck hole and volcanic peak and they saw many. They traveled from the jungles to 12,000 ft altitude. The car had a chance to prove its worth. Dwight

Goodenough, John's right hand man, just pulled back on the steering wheel and off they soared. They went from the dust of the dirt roads of Mexico to cobblestone streets of the highlands of the mountains of Guatemala."

The trip was broken up by a stopover in Mexico City where we were able to join Esther and Peggy for a few days of sightseeing. We met at the home of Rev. and Mrs. Harry Rosser, missionaries we had known in language school. They showed us the town. We saw the Aztec Pyramids and the Castle of Chapultepec where the emperor Maximilian and his wife Carlotta lived in lavish splendor. I was fearful that Esther would get some ideas about furnishing our new missionary home in Guatemala with crystal chandeliers, marble baths, and mother-of-pearl inlaid mahogany furniture but when we talked about what missionary life would be like we soon vetoed the idea. Then we visited Xochimilco, the Mexican floating gardens, but I was convinced that our patio was not large enough to have such a luxury. Besides there was not that much water in our humble old-fashioned missionary home in Quetzaltenango. The water only ran into the house for three hours each morning and the rest of the day, we had to get by with what we had been able to store in a 50 gallon drum placed on top of the wall. That height gave us gravity flow to the house as long as the water lasted. This made it a bit hard to take baths in the evening but we got by when we rationed the water.

Mexico, new to us, was a bit hard to get used to with its *mañana* lifestyle. Especially when we had to deal with the public officials at the borders and with the railroad officials.

For Esther and Peggy it was but a hop, skip and jump on the plane from Mexico City to Guatemala City. For Dwight and me it was an eleven day saga of very poor hotels and long days of driving on underdeveloped mountainous roads.

The next leg of the journey was from Mexico City to Oaxaca. The road was very difficult, full of curves, and often one way. Actually, it was the end of the road for the southern part of Mexico. There was a sort of dirt trail from there to Arriaga which we decided to take. Local residents assured us we would get through if we did not try to go too fast. We decided that it was used for ox carts — at least that is what it looked like. But we did make it. From there we followed the same trail to Tonolá which definitely was the end of the road. From there we had to put the car on a flat car of the railroad and wait for the train which seldom was on time. But we didn't know that. The railroad was the only way to get to the Guatemalan border so we had to take it.

We went to the railroad office to make arrangements for shipping the car on the next train that came through. After paying the official a large sum for shipping and another that served as a tip, we were told to load the car right away and when the train came through at 4:00 a.m. it would hook onto the flat car and take us to Tapachula which is on the Guatemalan border. That was good news. Next step was to find a way to load the car onto the flat car. There were no ramps, no lifts or other means of accomplishing that little task so we asked and asked. Finally we were told that a man over in the plaza had two, 2 by 12 planks that were often used for just that. Maybe we could convince him to stop his game of cards long enough to help us. After a lengthy negotiation and a big tip we got him to bring out his planks, which we laid at the end of the flat car. That meant we had to drive over the rails and line up the wheels on the planks. I was afraid to drive the car up onto the flat car because it all seemed too flimsy, but Dwight, bless his heart, was brave enough to try it. After quite a bit of adjusting and praying, the car was settled into position for the trip. But what would keep it in place for the 100-mile trip with all the jerking, starting and stopping of a freight train? The kind fellow came up with a solution: *maybe* he could find some ropes that might do the trick. And sure enough, with more tips and discussions, he produced some well-worn pieces that obviously had been used just for that purpose on a car that was returning north and had been unloaded just a day or two before at that same place. But, since the car owner had no way to get his ropes back to Tapachula, they were donated to this fellow. He kindly offered to tie the car down which he obviously had done several times for other tourists. That done, we settled in for the night in the back of the station wagon to get a good night's sleep.

Morning came and we were still in the station. No train had arrived, and after quite a bit of discussion, we discovered that the train had been held up by a piece of track that was unusable due to broken ties in the railroad bed. We went downtown for breakfast and then sat in the shade of a couple of trees in the plaza. Of course, soon there was a crowd of little curious boys wanting to know all about us and where we were going. One of them produced some lukewarm soft drinks which we bought and actually enjoyed. "When will the train come?" we asked them. "Soon" was about all they knew. The station master had told us that it should arrive by 10 AM but that hour was already past. "Maybe, Señor, it will come in the afternoon." But it did not come that afternoon and we had to wait till 4:00 a.m. the second day and finally, 24 hours later, we left the station.

"If all goes well," the brakeman told us, "we will be in Tapachula by midnight." What a relief, we were on our way with hopes of a good trip. We lay down again in the back of the car and were lulled to sleep by the rocking and clickity clak of the wheels on the iron rails. About 4:00 a.m. we realized that we had stopped and got up hurriedly ready to drive off the flat car and be on our way. They had told us there was a ramp in Tapachula station and we thought it meant we would soon be in Guatemala.

Not so! After dressing, we got down and began to check things out. We were not in the large town of Tapachula, but in a little pueblo of about 15 grass huts. Walking around in the dark we finally located the brakeman who was in one of the huts having coffee. "Where are we?" I asked him. He gave me the name but it meant nothing to us so I asked why we were on the siding with only three or four other flat cars. His reply was that the engine had run out of water and had gone to Tapachula alone to replenish the supply because it could not get there pulling the whole train. The brakeman assured us that it would be back soon and to be patient. He did not seem to be concerned so we accepted his explanation. Sure enough, in about six hours, it did return and hooked onto the flat cars and off we went. Five hours later, we actually arrived and looked out of the window of the car to see a large town and knew that it was Tapachula. As we checked our calendar, we realized it had only taken us from Sunday afternoon when we loaded the car onto the flat car until Wednesday 2:00 p.m. to travel the 100 or so miles.

We looked for the ramp, ready to unload the car and get on our way to the nice hotel in town where we could get a good meal and a bath. But there was no one around to give permission to move the flat car to the ramp. Finally, a little boy that was hanging around told us that the secret was to tip everyone. The workmen then began to show up. By giving 20 pesos to the railroad men, 10 to the customs agent, 10 to his helper, and 5 to the engineer we finally were able to get the car to the ramp and back on the ground. Two disgruntled fellows finally were able to drive up to the hotel where we had a good meal and a good night's sleep.

Dwight was anxious to get on our way so we had an early breakfast, filled the car with gas and were on our way to the border. Again we had a long wait. The Guatemalan authorities were very concerned with the hoof and mouth disease in Mexico and did not want anyone to bring it into the country. So we had to completely unload the car. They put all the baggage into a shack and made us wait for three hours while it was fumigated. Then they sprayed the car inside and out. Finally, with the approval of immigration, we were on our way. We were warned that we could not travel the regular coastal route because the flooding of 1949 had washed out the bridges and we would have to take the old road up the hill through San Marcos to Quetzaltenango. Most of the road had been leveled off with a bulldozer, but in some parts the only trail was where the river bottom was cleared of large boulders and smoothed so the cars and trucks could get through. It was a harrowing experience and often we wondered if we would hit bottom and break a hole in the pan or something. But with care and driving slowly, we finally arrived at the Wick's home near Quetzaltenango and a place to spend the night. The next day we slowly drove over the gravel road to Guatemala City and our new home. Esther and Peggy were waiting for us at the Thorp's home and it was with grateful hearts that we thanked God for a safe trip.

La Posada
Totonicapán, Guatemala, 1951

Our first experience with a Posada was in the Indian Pueblo of Totonicapán in the highlands of Guatemala. We lived in Quetzaltenango, but to get ready for Christmas we went to the capital city of Guatemala to buy our Christmas presents and some special goodies for the table. To get to Guatemala City, which is at 5,000 ft. altitude, one had to drive on dirt roads for about 125 miles over the cordillera where the road climbed up to about 12,000 feet. It was quite a drive and took about five hours over the winding road they called the *setenta vueltas*, referring to the 70 hairpin turns. Some were so sharp that we had to shift down to low to make the steep turn, especially when the car was full of people and their Christmas presents. Some old timers among the missionaries commented on my driving because when I drove alone, the trip took about three hours. But to make the trip that fast one had to be alone in the car

because the weight of several people was too much for the small motor and it almost came to a halt as we pulled through the sharp turns. This same trip was made by buggy when the first missionaries came to Guatemala and on one trip, the horse died because of the lack of air at the high altitude. The missionary turned the buggy over for a place for his wife to be safe and then walked to the next town to buy another horse.

We spent the day shopping in the capital city, and didn't start that long drive home until late in the afternoon. As we descended from the high peaks of the cordillera about 9:00 p.m. we came into Totonicapán, a Mayan Village with cobblestone streets. It was nice to get away from the dusty dirt road for a little while, even though the stones were quite rough, but it meant we were getting closer to home. The kids were asleep in the back seat, but suddenly they were awakened by a large procession marching along the main street filled with people. The people were all dressed in their Mayan costumes and marching along very slowly carrying a statue of Mary and Joseph on their shoulders. Even with the windows closed against the cold mountain night air, we could hear their native drums made from hollow tree trunks and sheep skins. One man played his homemade bamboo flute. They chanted weird tunes developed over the centuries by their Mayan culture. A strange hollow sound, which is characteristic of the posada, was the clicking sound from the striking of a turtle shell.

Of course, they didn't move over for a lonely car, for this

was a very important occasion, so we just followed along. The posada consists of villagers carrying statues of Joseph and Mary on their shoulders and chanting that they are looking for a place for the baby Jesus to be born. This religious custom is taken from the story of Jesus being born in a manger.

And Joseph went up from Galilee, out of the city of Nazareth, into Judea, unto the city of David, which is called Bethlehem to be taxed with Mary his espoused wife, being great with child. And so it was, that while they were there the days were accomplished that she should be delivered. And she brought forth her firstborn son, and wrapped him in swaddling clothes, and laid him in a manger; *because there was no room for them in the inn.* Luke 2:4-7

This is the setting for the *posadas*. The men carried a platform with the life size statues of the sacred couple, and called out at every home, "Does anyone have room for Joseph

and Mary, a place where they can spend the night, where the baby Jesus can be born?" They stopped at several houses and asked, "Is there room for the baby Jesus here?" No one seemed to have a place for Him. After about 15 minutes, they arrived at a pre-selected home and the owners ran out and invited Joseph and Mary to come in. *They had room in their home! Room for the parents of Jesus and a place for Jesus to be born.* They invited those carrying the statues, as well as the whole crowd, into their home. We probably would have been welcome too, but didn't ask because we wanted to get home.

But that is when the whole event lost its sacred significance. The statues were placed in a dark corner with one lighted candle, no longer important and completely ignored. The table was set with tamales wrapped in banana leaves, which is a great delicacy and eaten with bread and coffee and replaces the regular menu of tortillas and black beans. Lots of festivities followed with heavy drinking and partying. The poor holy couple and their son Jesus were inconvenient and pushed off into a dark corner. It didn't take long for our children to comment that it didn't seem to them that there was any room for Jesus at that *Posada.*

Now the road had cleared and we were on our way. As we drove home, the chorus that we used to sing in Christian Endeavor came to our minds, and we sang it together as we drove off into the lonely night, "Into my heart, into my heart, come into my heart, Lord Jesus. Come in today, come in to stay, come into my heart, Lord Jesus."

Christmas in Guatemala
Quetzaltenango, Guatemala, 1952

December 30

Dearest family,

This letter should be dated a day later: here's why! I got the date put on the paper and someone came in . . . Then it was time to bathe and feed Phyllis: then it was time to fix lunch: then I took a siesta for the first time in weeks: then it was time to feed Phyllis: then . . . and so it goes. See what you are in for, Jean!

Well, we have come thru Christmas with flying colors, and we only need New Year's day to top it off. Very shortly before Christmas, I was named choir director and from then on, every spare moment was spent in practice, and some spare moments were not to be found. I was wrapping gifts until after midnight, and I did not get the wreath up over the fireplace until two days after Christmas. The program at the church on Christmas Eve went off without too many hitches. It was supposed to start at 7:30. At 8:00 p.m. I went to start playing the prelude, and the organ would not work. It is electric. I turned on the switch but the pedal and the stops would not work. Just then, the master of ceremonies came around to see why I had not started the prelude. He called John out of the audience and he and the pastor had it fixed in about 20 minutes. Then the children and the young people put on several short pieces, the pastor preached for 15 minutes, and there were two pageants. They cut out whole scenes of the second one because it was so late that people were leaving. We finished at 11:30. From there the people go to have dinner and then have their tree and gifts just at midnight. The Catholics say that Christ was born at midnight so they shoot off fire crackers and celebrate at that hour. We came home and filled the children's stockings. I had sewed some big red and green stockings out of felt with trees and candy canes on them. They should last the rest of our lives. After that, I went into the bedroom and the girls and John brought out my gift. For two weeks, he had been sawing and pounding away all day and some of the night too. Now I have the loveliest desk and sewing table! It is light wood, streamlined, drawers on one side and a big slab on the other side instead of legs. A panel comes out of the top and the sewing machine sets in flush with the table top. It is such a nice looking piece of furniture that we are going to keep it in the living room.

That was the beginning of Christmas day for us. The men's prayer group which we had started a few months ago had planned a family picnic for that day at the lake, but they could not get transportation at the last minute, so we had to invite them to come to our house and be 'gringos' for the day in an old fashioned barbeque. We had just finished our outdoor fireplace. It has a bench on each side, a chimney and a metal plate at the back to keep things hot. We served weenies to over 80 people, almost half of them children, and had no trouble at all. We had a grill over the embers and cooked 20 weenies at a time. The people lined up; we gave them their dishes and weenies on one side; they went over to the other side for buns, mustard, potato salad and drinks, and we got along fine. They didn't like the idea of pickles and did not take them. Several ladies asked me for the recipe for the salad. It did not have any pickles in it, but they didn't know the difference. We ordered 200 rolls, but I didn't send down for them until the afternoon of the day before, and had not paid for them so the bakery sold them to somebody else!

Next scene: me up at 6:00 a.m. (I usually get up at 6:30) making four batches of dough in hopes that it will make 200 rolls. It did! The pastor's two teenage daughters came over and helped. Guess what we made the salad in - the little washing machine tub we got from the States! It was so full that she could not stir it and had to put some of it into the large wash basin. Then we put it all into the latter, piled high, and made lemonade in the former. It was worth all the work, because it made us popular with many of the brethren whom we had not known very well before. We are finding that it pays to take time to be friendly with the folks here even though our work assignment is mostly in other parts of the country. They responded to us so readily.

I was glad this didn't get sent yesterday, as your composite family letter arrived last night from Highland Park. Wish we could have been there. Our family Christmases are always so much fun and I miss them terribly. The missionaries in Quetzaltenango station usually get together for dinner on Christmas day but could not get around to it this year so we are having dinner on the 2nd out at the Wicks home in San Cristobal at the Quiché Bible Institute. The Wicks just got back from Guatemala City. They had a baby girl on the 19th of Dec. So this way they could be included in the missionary party. The Methodist family will join us for they live at the Institute also and that will make 26 of us.

We put the Santa you sent Freddy on the mantle along with some choir boy candles and a large candle under the wreath. The tree decorated is at the top. We stapled all of our cards to the wall and our home looks very festive. I know you had a wonderful Christmas with the family. We will be home two years from now. Charlotte has two teeth at last. We are well.

Love, Esther

Driving to Guatemala with the Family
1952

We had been home to the USA for a short furlough in order to obtain permanent visas for Guatemala. Charlotte was ready for this world and Esther went to the Hollywood Presbyterian Hospital so that the baby could be born in style. The visa came in early December and we said good bye to our family and friends, anxious to get home to Quetzaltenango where we could celebrate Christmas in our Guatemalan home. There had been a delay getting the new baby on Esther's passport but she would not listen to the idea of leaving Charlotte at the border. The Lord was good to us. We got the passport back in time, and were soon on our way.

The Pan American highway came to an end more than four hundred kilometers from the Guatemalan border so, as on our previous trip, the car had to be shipped on a flat car of the Mexican train. It was fortunate that they connected the flat car to the passenger train which was much faster than the freight train. We had hoped to sleep in the car, but the authorities had just passed a new law that no one could ride in an automobile that was mounted on a flat car.

From a letter Esther sent home March, 1952

Dearest family,

We have been back for almost three months! It scarcely seems possible, yet here we are, not yet completely unpacked because there were so many conferences and meetings waiting for us. We arrived the week before Christmas with a new baby and Pep and Fred still very small children. Still, we just had to have a Christmas tree. Since none was available in the plaza, John just cut branches from the cypress shrubs in the patio and nailed them to the wall in the corner of our living room, right next to the fireplace. It was decorated in the evening after the children had gone to bed and next morning they accepted it as the real thing.

Upon arriving there was an evangelistic meeting John had to lead, young people's Christmas programs at the church to organize, innumerable trips to visit churches on the Pacific Coast and a youth convention to organize at Bethel Church here in Quetzaltenango. Would you please pray for many youth to accept Christ at this special meeting we are organizing for the 22nd of March?

We had no trouble getting into Mexico even though we were pulling a teardrop trailer that John and his dad had built on our short furlough. We, who had grown up in Southern California, had forgotten how cold it can get in some parts of the States in December and had quite a time pulling the trailer through a snow storm as we crossed the continental divide in New Mexico.

In the country of Mexico, we sailed down the Pan-American Highway, making every effort to enjoy it because we knew that in Guatemala the roads were very difficult because many bridges had been washed out by the devastating heavy rains and floods of 1949. Most of the roads had been destroyed or were limited to a temporary dirt surface. To cross the rivers we either had temporary log bridges or had to drive right through the streams. We were not entirely in agreement with the Mexican guide book which said: "Mexico's highway engineers, departing from the old custom of constructing roads through valleys, chose to build highways along the sides and ridges of the country's towering mountains." We found that the highways truly were mountain roads with many curves and steep grades. Many times, we had to shift into low to get over some of the high mountains. Sometimes the road was alongside a steep precipice or next to a deep canyon and quite scary because of no side rails. These roads are beautiful but sometimes we wished they had not been quite so unconventional.

At Arriaga, which is on the tropical hot coastal plain, the road comes to its end; from there one has to put the car on a flat car and go by train. The last few miles had been over oxcart trails but we finally arrived at the town just at dusk to find the accommodations very primitive. The hotel looked as bad as it smelled so we drove around until we found a small Nazarene

Church with a fenced yard. After a prayer, we asked the native pastor and his family if we could park in the patio for the night and sleep on the benches of the church. When they learned we were missionaries they readily offered us anything they had, which was very little. We settled for a few tortillas and then got out our bottled water and a couple of cans of food we had in the trailer. We prepared our supper over the G.I. stove of our trailer, moving it to one of their Sunday School rooms. The girls slept in the trailer and the boys on benches in the church.

The next day the car and trailer were driven up some wide planks onto the flat car and soon we were on our way to the town of Tapachula, which is right on the border of Guatemala. We were obligated to ride "First Class" in one of the passenger cars since no one was allowed to ride in the car. Fortunately, it was a passenger train and made good time though we commented that we would have been more comfortable in the car and trailer. Charlotte was about two months old and when she needed her bottle, I had to sit on the bottle for at least 15 minutes to warm the milk so she would drink it. We arrived at the end of our train trip about 2:00 a.m. and after "many tips," they accommodated us by unloading the car and trailer within the hour. From the railroad station and freight yard we drove the few blocks to the hotel where we were able to get some nice rooms. I dare say it was the nicest shower that I have ever had!

Early the next morning we were on our way to the border

crossing. At the Guatemala border, they were very kind and thoughtful when they saw we had children with us and pushed us right through immigration. How grateful we were for the prayers of all of you for a safe trip through Mexico and no hang-ups at the border into Guatemala. A few blocks later, we came to the customs house and they didn't even look into the trailer. Maybe it was that they were all very excited. They reported to us that there had been a coup during the night and there was rioting in the streets of the capital city. The border guards had just received word that they were ordered to close the border! We had just made it and were the last car to get into Guatemala! *How wonderful to think that God had allowed us to get there just in time.* Otherwise, we would have had to spend the next two weeks in the little hot tropical town of Tapachula with three very small children and prices rising every day until the border opened two weeks later.

The roads in Guatemala were just as bad as we had expected. The coastal road, which normally is the best route, was not open yet for there were many deep rivers to cross and some of the bridges were out. We had to drive up the river valley and steep range to San Marcos and then over the highlands to our home in Quetzaltenango at 8,000 feet elevation. In one place, they routed us across a railroad bridge where we bounced up and down between the ties. But we made it! The road was very steep and even normally was very serious driving. But after the flooding, a bulldozer had simply run along the edge of a stream and leveled the area, removing the rocks, to make an improvised road. Most of the time we had to drive in low. Trucks and rain are not a very good combination on that kind of road and we often feared we would get stuck in the potholes made by the big trucks; but we made it. One time we looked back to discover that the bouncing had worked the trailer hitch loose and we had to go back some ways to get it. We did get badly stuck in one spot where they were working on the road but there were workmen who were glad to push us through the holes and mud for a fee. It will probably be finished by the time the rains start again.

Home surely looked good; the house was all clean and ready and we were most thankful to the Lord who had brought us safely back to Quetzaltenango. *Gratefully we thanked God again for His many wonderful miracles that brought us home safely!"*

Burning the Devil
Guatemala City, Guatemala, 1970

They are burning the devil tonight! One of the popular holiday traditions of Guatemala is the religious custom of *Quemando el Diablo*. Every December 7th at 6:00 p.m. exactly, many of the streets of the city have bonfires out in front of homes. This is the official beginning of the Christmas season. The size of the bonfire depends on the means of the family. The fires are supposed to burn up the Devil. How nice it would be if it were only that easy. It is interesting that this year, 1970, the country was still under a "state of siege," but the government found a way to put through a special decree permitting firecrackers and these bonfires so the citizens could carry out this religious custom.

Over 50 percent of the population is Mayan Indian. Many still dress in their native customs and speak a local dialect of the Mayan race. There are over 22 distinct Mayan Indian tribes, each with its own language. Archeological studies inform us that this civilization began over 2,000 years ago in the highlands of what is now Guatemala City. Actually, one of the oldest pyramids and oldest ruins are right in the middle of the capital city. The name of this ruin is Kaminal Juyú and this suburb of the city has the same name. Archeological diggings have found that there are three or four distinct epochs of construction of this pyramid. The new ruler just built a higher and better one on top of the older one. It is suggested that each ruler was more famous and more important, so he increased the size and height of the last pyramid to establish his position.

From the highlands of Guatemala, the civilization moved to the eastern coastal plains and built Tikal which is famous today as one of the largest and best preserved of all Mayan sites. Another important site is Copan, built in northern Honduras. In Southern Mexico there are other ruins of Mayan pyramids and cities, including Chichen Itzá. The Mayan network covered most of the area from northern Honduras to the Yucatán Peninsula. . They are a major part of Central America. Some are still being discovered in the dense jungles of northern Guatemala and in the department of Chiapas, southern Mexico.

The Mayan culture has many pagan practices and beliefs. As

the Conquistadores settled in Central America, they established the first Spanish capital in 1541, now known as Antigua Guatemala. From there they conquered the New World beginning with Central America and Mexico. The soldiers and priests of Spain overcame the Mayas, but were not able to integrate many of them into their lifestyle, into their religion or into their church. Many did submit to the church and worshiped in the new cathedrals, which were sometimes built on top of Mayan temple sites. They were willing to be baptized and took on the Catholic religious customs. Those who were converted took on the Spanish customs and way of life but still kept their old stone gods, adapting this new religion into their old beliefs.

A good example can be found in the churches of the town of Chichicastenango, which were built on top of old worship sites of the early Mayans. Their pyramids were built as ceremonial centers where they ruled, studied the constellations and worshiped the stars, among other things. Many of the new converts simply went into the churches, which now occupied the same location as their old sites, to burn candles and say their prayers, in the native Mayan language. The church in Chichicastenango has no benches and the floor is covered with candles lit in worship. On the steps of the church the modern day witch doctors still swing their lighted incense burners, some made of sardine cans, and repeat in Maya Quiché their own pagan prayers mingled with the new ones they have been taught.

When they came to the knowledge of the existence of a devil, they incorporated this teaching into the yearly celebrations as part of the Christmas festival and today, still *burn the devil*. But this simple act has nothing to do with our understanding of the role of the devil as it is taught in the Scriptures. We know from the Bible that the devil is a supremely evil being, the prince of the power of the air. Jesus came to destroy the works of the devil and end the conflict between good and evil. It all came to a head in Christ's death on the cross when He conquered death and was resurrected from the dead.

The tradition of burning the devil, mixed with Mayan culture and religious teaching, has the temporal effect of making some think that it is possible to eliminate the devil with a simple ceremony once a year. For a week or more, everyone, even in the large cities, gathers sticks and firewood along with old newspapers. Then, at dusk on December 7, they take their loot out into the center of the street in front of their homes and start the fire that is supposed to *burn up the devil*. One can imagine how soon the city fills with this temporary light and smoke, not to mention the smell. It is all in hopes that they will keep the devil under control for another year. Wouldn't it be great if it were that simple?

Deputation Teams
Monte Sión, Guatemala, 1964

Dearest Families,

The summer is almost over, and it is time that I wrote you all, so please forgive the carbon copies - - it is the only way that I can get a letter off to each of you. You will see why.

I guess that we could say that the summer began when Peggy came home from the USA. She brought Carol Zimmer with her who stayed a little over a month. She is a lovely girl, and we enjoyed having her. Of course, it has been wonderful having Peggy here too. A week after Peggy arrived, Janet and Phyllis came home from the Mission School in Quetzaltenango. Fred and Charlotte did not get here until August 12. So now we have the family all together. But we are not alone! There are 19 university students here from various USA churches that came as work teams.

We have had varying numbers of university students from the States since the middle of June. At first, four came from Seattle University Church. Two of them went to stay with the Winters in Ostuncalco, near Quetzaltenango. They worked there for three weeks, while the other two stayed with us. Mary Joe is a certified lifesaving instructor and taught Chema the rudiments of lifesaving and she also taught Char, Phyllis, and Janet to dive.

Chema did well enough that she could give him a lifesaving certificate. What a boon to the camp! We have operated without a life guard since the beginning. Mary Joe also started a small girls club in the church in Amatitlán. The other student did the same for the boys and also helped in the Sunday services. He knew only a few phrases in Spanish but he could really communicate. He wasn't afraid to try, and has a smile that won everyone. Then came four students from San Diego. [This group included Don Weisbrod, who later created and organized Icthus, a Christian club program for the children in our churches.] There was also a girl from New Jersey, so I had 9 extra children to look after. The first week they had orientation, had visits from a representative from the Bible Society and Wycliffe Bible Translators. Bob Thorp came and spoke to them one afternoon about the work of the Presbyterian Church in Guatemala. (Bob is the chairman of the mission). They did a Bible study together each morning in the lodge, which our children usually attended. We took them to visit the American Embassy where they met Mr. Lobenstene, economic advisor to the ambassador, and a very good friend to missions, having been a "mish kid" himself in China. They also met with a Christian layman who is high up in the cultural attaché's office.

The big project for them this summer was to be counselors in the camp at *Monte Sión* sponsored by the Union Church (our English-speaking Protestant Church in the city). It wasn't easy for some of the university students to see this as missionary work but we explained that these are "poor little rich kids." We could see afterwards that many of the campers learned just what it means to be a Christian. This camp was for three weeks and we all were glad when it was over because it was tiring to keep going that long without a break.

I have not had to prepare meals for the university gang those weeks as they ate with the camp in the dining room, which has an excellent cook who speaks English, Jamaica style. The students loved him and often talked about their lives and cultures with him. I do seem to end up doing all the washing for the university gang and it keeps me and the maid busy. The girls do their own ironing as do my daughters, the smaller ones as much as they can, and they do flat work which helps. The first two weeks of camp, it rained constantly, and everything was very muddy. The university gang was in and out of the house constantly, and they had varying degrees of tummy aches, colds, bites etc. Doctor Ainsley was on call, and we had a camp nurse, but I did all of the mothering!

In August, Tom Merick and Newel Hendricks arrived from the Glendale Church. One of the groups in that church had donated a public address system to be installed in the cabins and throughout the camp in strategic spots to make announcements and wake-up calls. Tom was studying electronics; in fact, he is going to Moody Bible Institute in the fall, and he was able to supervise the entire installation with Newel's help. Newel had experience in surveying and prepared a map of the property that allows us to identify all the underground systems and wires: something John had been wanting for a long time.

The Seattle kids left a week ago, so from feeding 18 people I am down to 14 now. In a couple of days, the San Diego gang will leave, then there will be only three extra until September 4th, when the rest leave. This week I have not had to do the cooking, but turned it over to Deman, the camp cook. The kids have been digging ditches for the sound system wires and the girls have been varnishing the doors of the cabins and painting. Some have been able to do some secretarial work. One nice thing we did for them was to go on a caravan with four of the Guatemala university students to see the rural Presbyterian Churches and take part in their services as well as visit some of the tourist sites like Chichicastenango and Lake Atitlán. They also were invited to attend some of the activities of the Student University Group (ACU) meetings in the city that Bob and Bernice Thorp direct.

Now a little bit about the family. The most important thing is that Fred has graduated from the 8th grade. Very conveniently, the university students were in the city at the time so we could leave and go to the graduation in Huehue without worrying about them. Peggy didn't want to go with us which seemed strange, but she had visited the school earlier with Carol. However, she has been running the camp store in the lodge for all the camps, and there was to be a camp that week. It was the annual meeting of the Friends Mission. One of the girls had been a pal of Peggy's while she attended the missionary school at Huehuetenango, so she had company. We were to be gone only two days. The big factor was that the university students were to climb the volcano Pacaya on Wednesday, which was the graduation day, and she didn't want to miss going to the volcano since she missed the first climb because she was on a tourist trip with Carol. It was really a hard decision to make, yet when we got back, she said that she wouldn't have missed climbing the live volcano for anything. They started about 3 a.m. and saw the sunrise from the top as well as the tops of many of the other volcanoes in the country.

After getting the missionaries from the Friends Mission all settled on Monday we left that evening and drove along the Pacific coast to San Felipe and stopped at the Emery's home. Their two oldest are home for the summer, but had gone up to Huehue for the graduation so John and I had their beds, and they put up cots for Phyllis and Janet. Phyllis has given herself a nickname. She now calls herself Phee! I don't really know how to spell it, as it is the first letter of her name in the Greek alphabet. Her teacher in Quetzaltenango taught her how to spell her name in Greek and she signs all her letters that way now! Janet has learned the Greek alphabet too, but it did not interest her that much. Now Phyllis has learned the whole Greek alphabet just for fun. What good it will do her, I don't know, but I'm proud of her for being interested. We arrived at Huehue at noon. In the afternoon, there was the annual recital. Some trumpets and a violin besides piano pieces. The first and second graders gave a poem as a voice choir. It was very well done. In the evening, they gave the *HMS Pinafore*. Different children took turns reading the narrative, while the actors pantomimed the speaking parts. The 7th graders took the solo parts. Charlotte was Josephine. The beauty in this particular operetta is that all the children could take part, the boys as Jack Tars and the girls as Sisters and Cousins and Aunts. It was very well done and everyone was congratulated, especially the teachers who pounded the music into them.

On Wednesday, the graduation began at ten. There were several special numbers by the graduates, vocal and instrumental. This was the 30th anniversary of the school so they celebrated that too. The principal had come 28 years ago as a missionary teacher. She was the teacher of the 7th and 8th grades, but she gave the privilege of handing out the diplomas to another teacher who had been this class's first grade teacher. The man who gave the sermon was the father of one of the graduates. His first daughter had been a pupil in the school when it first started, and now on the 30th anniversary his youngest daughter was graduating. There were five girls and three boys graduating, the largest in the history of the school. Fourteen of the children who have gone through Huehue or attended the school are now on the mission field. Afterwards the whole crowd went out to the patio and everyone took pictures. We headed for home right after lunch as it is a long drive, and many of the roads are gravel and over high mountains.

You wouldn't know Fred and Charlotte. They have grown so much this year. One of the 8th graders decided early in June that she would fatten Freddy up, so she promised him 50 cents if he would get up to 105 lbs. by graduation. Everyone cooperated and passed him all the extra food. He made it and now we can't fill him up! He is as tall as I am now. Charlotte cut her hair, one of the mothers at the school knew how to follow the natural wave, and it is just beautifully curly. She is almost, 5 feet 3 inches. Peggy and I have been giving sewing lessons to Charlotte, Phyllis and Janet this last week or two, and they are doing just fine. We have certainly enjoyed having them home. Peggy is going to stay till the middle of next week so we can have the family alone for a few days. Fred will go to the Missionary High School in Quetzaltenango in October with Janet and Phyllis. They now have a 9th grade. You can imagine how busy John has been supervising and working with all these work teams.

Love from us all.
Esther

GOD'S PROVISION

Robbed at Gun Point
Barranquilla, Colombia, 1946

When we were the new missionaries in Columbia and John was assigned to the Sinú Valley which kept him away from home for six weeks at a time, Esther and two month old Peggy were asked to live in Barranquilla temporarily in a house that the mission had rented for living quarters for the missionaries. The combined rent allowance was enough to pay for the building and a youth center. This was the only way the mission could have a youth center. The huge house consisted of more than fifteen rooms. There was a large reception area in the front that was used for youth meetings and games. This area had been offices and reception for a private hospital and was quite large and ideal for them. Three missionary families had agreed to live in what had been private rooms each having its own bath. Some of the rooms were interconnected so that two of the missionary families had two personal rooms. These families had their rooms on one side of the patio and the new Shackelford missionaries were assigned to take one of the single rooms on the other side. The house had a

large patio in the center and the rooms were built all around this central area. There was a dining room large enough for all three families to eat together in a sort of dormitory style. The missionary wives took turns supervising the cooking and the maintenance. The upstairs apartment was rented to an English couple, which gave us a bit more financial help.

This is Esther's letter home to her family about the robbery and her trauma with the armed thieves:

Today I'll finish this letter or know the reason why! I've been holding it up to tell you about something that I haven't wanted to write about at night, because it still frightens me, yet I must tell you before you hear from another source.

On Tuesday night, early in June, I was particularly late feeding Peggy — or early since I finished about 2 a.m. I heard a noise as though the front door latch were closing. I waited a few moments and heard nothing more. I was curious so went out in my bare feet and nighty to investigate. I really didn't think of robbers, so when I saw a figure in the sewing room, it didn't register until too late. The man came toward me with a revolver in one hand and a knife in the other telling me to be quiet. Under these circumstances, one does as told and especially in this country where robbers think nothing of hurting or even killing. Then another man appeared and assured me that if I kept quiet they would not hurt me. They said there were three more outside of the house, they had escaped from jail and all they wanted was money. All I had was five pesos which they soon found. Actually I hadn't any more, fortunately, I guess. They took John's good chronograph watch, which he would not take on these trips for fear of its being stolen, and they took mine also. They both happened to be on the table. They saw our good camera but didn't take it! One man stayed with me while the other started looking through the rest of the house. He got over to the other side of the patio just as Ellen got up to go to the bathroom and saw him and called to Ted her husband. She kept crying out and finally screamed. I was so afraid that he would hurt her since she was eight months pregnant. But Ted shouted at the man and called for Dick, the other missionary husband. I guess the commotion was too much for the robbers and they ran out including my guard. I was afraid they would return with the rest of the men so I ran out to warn the others. But nothing more happened. After we had talked it over we went back to bed, but of course, I couldn't get to sleep.

I know that the Lord was protecting me. The men could have done me physical harm, especially since all I had on was a thin nighty. I'm sure that they were really what they said they were because when he picked up John's watch he said, "This will help us on the journey." I begged him not to take it and he said, "Where's the money?" When I said I hadn't any, he put the watch in his pocket with the promise to give it back if he found money. I almost think he might have done it.

The funny part about it all was the whispered conversation I had with my guard. At first, I picked up Peggy to bubble her, though really more for support, since she was sound asleep. The man watched me for a moment, and then said, "Why don't you sit down?" and patted the pillow on the chair. Presently I put Peggy back in the crib and sat down again.

He squatted on the floor and started asking questions, "Where is your husband?"

"In Cereté."

"Aren't you happy with him?"

"Oh yes."

"What business is your husband in?"

"He's a missionary." He didn't quite understand.

Finally he said, "On a mission for the government?"

"No, he's a missionary of the Protestant Church."

"Oh, does he take pictures?"

"Yes."

"Isn't he a German spy?"

"What?"

"Aren't all missionaries German spies?"

"No!" I said with an inflection which meant, "What a foolish idea." You see, we were really getting chummy! Later he asked if I wasn't afraid. I guess most Colombian women would have been in a state of collapse. At first I was shaking but got hold of myself when the men didn't do anything to me. After I sat down, I was really quite relaxed. Perhaps too much so, for the saddest part is yet to come. The man saw my diamond flashing, took it off and put in his pocket. I begged him not to take it but didn't dare resist too much. The police came the next day and recognized my description of the men. Nothing has been reported and I don't suppose we will get anything back. The robbers went out the sewing room door, but we are not sure yet how they got in since nothing looks jimmied.

Will you tell Auntie and Daddy about it? I couldn't write even to John for a week and even now I feel weak in the knees thinking about it. I've gotten over most of my nervousness at night. But I go through the whole thing again every time I write about it; I would rather not have to think about it anymore.

This all has kept me hopping and so I have had very little time for letters, I'm sorry to say. There are so many to write.

Loving you, Esther

Going To Jail
Quetzaltenango, Guatemala, 1952

How often we are so busy we forget to wait on the Lord and trust in Him. Often my pride led me to think I could do it all by myself. I just didn't take time to look for His will and His way for my life, thinking I was perfectly capable of doing everything by myself because I was so capable. Many times, He had to show me that I was not able in myself and just slow me down so I would put my trust in Him. That is what happened when the authorities put me in jail in Quetzaltenango, Guatemala.

When we first arrived in Guatemala the roads were mostly gravel or dirt and rather primitive. Travel was slow even on the main arteries. However, after World War II, when other countries began to help build the Pan American Highway, Guatemala was soon to have its road paved from border to border. The road from our home in Quetzaltenango to San Cristobal was part of the main highway to Guatemala City and was paved as far as the Quiché Bible Institute, so we were able to drive faster over that 15 kilometers. Don Pablo and doña Dora Burgess were veteran missionaries who founded the school for the Quiché speaking people, since there was no public school for them in their own language. Stan and Betty Wick lived there and taught the Maya Quiché Indian youth who had been converted under their ministry.

Stan often asked me to come out to the Institute to lend a hand, for he and Betty had specialized in academics, teaching in the Quiché language, and Stan had little experience in mechanics. So they turned to me since I had grown up on the farm and had been taught to keep gasoline motors running. Stan and Betty had no electricity or phone and had to rely on gasoline motors and kerosene lanterns. Betty wanted to do the wash one morning, but no matter how many times Stan pumped the kick starter it would not start. Unknown to Stan, he had flooded the engine. We lived in Quetzaltenango at the time, and when Stan sent word of his problem, Peggy and I jumped in the car and drove out to help. By the time we got there, the flooded carburetor had dried out. All that was necessary was to give the kick starter one push and the motor started right up. No doubt, simple things like that were what gave me the reputation of being an engineer. This only added to my feeling of importance that I could do anything. Human pride, I guess.

The road back to Quetzaltenango was not a freeway. First, you pass through the town of Salcajá, the town famous for its tie and dye weaving by the Quiché Indians. They hang the tied thread on the barbed wire fence along the road to dry and it is quite a sight. After you leave that town there is a straightaway where one can actually go about 70 *kilometros* or 45 miles an hour. Peggy and I were in a hurry to get home and were traveling about that fast when I saw an Indian farmer with a huge native hoe on his shoulder. He was walking along the edge of the pavement and watching the car. Just as we got next to him, he suddenly turned and tried to run across the road right in front of us. Did the car surprise him or was he afraid of a vehicle that came racing toward him? I found out later it had to do with a belief in evil spirits of the Mayan Indian religion. The car must have left about 40 feet of skid marks but the poor Indian did not run fast enough and the bumper of the car broke his leg, though by then we had almost stopped. I ran over to see what we could do for him, but he only spoke the Indian language of which I did not know more than a word or two. It did not take me long to realize I was in trouble. Finally, Peggy and I realized that there was nothing we could do but pray, because that was a really helpless situation and I suddenly was not in charge anymore.

God reached out to me and Peggy. It is a great experience to have your children show you how simple childlike faith and assurance can make a difference. Soon the Lord sent a car that served as a bus and whose chauffeur and owner was a member of our church in Salcajá that we had just passed. He offered to go to the town phone and call the ambulance in Quetzaltenango, and then he drove over to the Quiché Bible Institute to tell Stan what had happened. The ambulance and Stan arrived at the accident about the same time. Again the Lord met our need, for the driver of the ambulance was a friend who attended the men's Bible study we had organized at the Bethel Church in Quetzaltenango. He took over and told me he would care for the man, take him to the hospital, and then go to our home to advise Esther what had happened and tell her where we were. Stan warned Peggy and me that it was a serious thing to have an accident when someone was hurt and that they would probably put me in jail. An officer had come in the ambulance, which I guess is standard procedure. After the ambulance had gone he got into our car, and sure enough ordered me to go straight to jail. By then Esther had arrived at the jail to take Peggy home and to pray with me.

By then it was late in the afternoon. Still, God was sending help. Another close friend and neighbor, Oscar Casteñeda, came to the jail to see how he could help me. Interestingly enough, they neither put me in a cell, nor handcuffed me. I was ordered to sit in a chair in the office of the police chief. Maybe it was because I was a missionary, who knows? Again, the Lord was there to look after me for those jails are not that elegant. About half an hour later, the chief of police came in and Oscar had a lengthy conversation with him. I didn't realize it but Oscar owned one of the bus companies that made the eight hour daily run to Guatemala City and knew all the important people in town. He explained that I was from the church, a good citizen and friend, and that he recommended that I be released into his custody. The chief turned to me and said that I could go home under Oscar's supervision, but I was to be back next morning.

Oscar then told me that I was not at liberty, but that I was obligated to stay in town until the judge would try the case. That often took months, but again the Lord intervened and, through Oscar, the judge was convinced to try the case the next day. So I was allowed to sleep at home, but had to report to the office of the chief of police at 8:00 each morning. It was an interesting day. It was a short walk to his office. My car was impounded, and since the police budget was rather limited, they did not have any transportation but depended on public buses. About noon, the chief told me I could go home for lunch but I would have to take a policeman along to be sure I did not run away. Again, Oscar showed up and took us in his car, as he did not want me to suffer the indignity of walking the streets with a police escort. The policeman quietly and courteously sat in the living room, which was an extension of the dining room, while I had something to eat. Our children, Peggy and little Freddy, were intrigued to have a policeman in the house and made friends at once. They sat in his lap and played with his hat, for he was very friendly. I am sure that they helped my case considerably. We served him coffee and dessert which he enjoyed greatly, as his profession does not pay well and he did not often have more than tortillas, black beans and coffee for his noon meal. I suppose we should have invited him to the table, but somehow it did not quite seem to fit into the culture. He probably would have rejected such a suggestion anyway.

After returning to the jail and office of the chief of police, I sat and read until about the middle of the afternoon. It was nice not to be locked up in a cell, but a feeling of helplessness was beginning to overcome me. And the cause of the accident kept coming back to me. Why had the man run in front of the car? What had I done wrong? This time of reflection again drove me to some serious time of silent prayer.

Bless his heart, again Oscar came over from his office and talked to the Judge. I didn't know they were friends. The first step in the trial was to investigate the accident personally. We got into Oscar's car with the judge and drove out to the scene of the accident, where Oscar took over as though he were the defense lawyer. He explained I had just come from the rough dirt streets of Salcajá and could not be going fast. Then he pointed out the skid marks which showed evasive action, and explained that I had tried to miss the farmer but he had turned and run in front of the car. I cannot testify to the truth of his explanation, but the judge nodded his head when Oscar reminded him that often, when the Indians are worried about something, they think an evil spirit is following them. If they run in front of a car, just close enough, the car would kill the evil spirit, but they had to run close so as not to be hit themselves. The judge accepted the explanation and asked us to drive him back to the office. This short trial was another miracle from the Lord using our friend Oscar to get it done. Things just don't move that fast under the judicial system that was adopted from Spain, where one is considered guilty until he can prove his innocence. The prisoner is not free to take part for he is always in the cell awaiting sentence. But the lawyer or the family has to gather the evidence, which takes weeks or sometimes months.

When we arrived at the judge's office, he had me sign some papers, and Oscar, as a witness, also signed; then I was a free man. Oscar took me home in his car, and the incident didn't even get into the evening papers. Next day I went back to pick up the car.

I was not able to converse with the man I hit because of the language, but visited him in the hospital. Stan went to see him and they had a long talk about the Lord and evil spirits. We were allowed to take him things to eat and prayed with him even though it was in Spanish. What great care and protection the Lord gave us on the mission field and He often used native believers to intercede for us and make His ministry a success in Guatemala.

Caught in a Revolution
Colomba, Guatemala, 1954

When assigned to be the director of youth work for the
Synod of Guatemala, one of my assignments was to help create
and develop a Christian Endeavor youth program in each of the
50 Presbyterian Churches of the Synod. We were living in
Guatemala City and both Esther and I were asked to teach in the
Presbyterian Seminary. At that time, the seminary had an
excellent quartet. One of the seminary students was from a
bilingual family. His father was from England and spoke English
as his native language and his mother was born a Guatemalan and
spoke Spanish as her native tongue; so this son was perfectly bilingual. He had an excellent education and felt drawn to the
ministry. He told us how he often listened to the short wave
Gospel Radio Station, HCJB, Quito, Ecuador. The preaching of
Donald Grey Barnhouse of the Tenth Presbyterian Church of
Philadelphia was his favorite. He listened to these programs
every night because he loved Dr. Barnhouse's Bible teachings on
the Book of Romans. But he also wanted to polish up his English
and soon began to sound like Dr. Barnhouse. He became the fifth
member of the quartet as the speaker.

We enlisted this team to help develop the youth program and
they were a valuable asset. There were youth conventions and

evangelistic meetings almost every weekend. The youth in the churches quickly responded to hearing the seminary quintet; the attendance was excellent wherever we went. Of course this helped the youth work grow and gain credence with the pastors and churches of the Synod. This speaker gave excellent evangelistic messages, even though sometimes he sounded like Donald Grey Barnhouse with a Spanish accent. These conventions and crusades led many to make decisions for Christ.

There were five Presbyteries in the Synod and each had a Christian Endeavor District. As often as we could we had these District leaders organize and supervise the conventions and we supported their efforts as speakers and musicians. Soon all of the Departments of Guatemala where there were Presbyterian Churches were holding public rallies. Invitations came from other Missions also. Next was organized a National Christian Endeavor Convention with International participation. It was held at the Central Presbyterian Church of Guatemala City. Rev. Ellis Shaw, the Executive Director of the California State Christian Endeavor Union, was our main speaker and leaders from the International Society Headquarters came to observe and take part.

The years of conventions and evangelistic meetings throughout the five Presbyteries produced great interest in Christian Endeavor summer youth camps. The attendance was overwhelming and the quartet was a major part of this program also. On one of these itinerary trips, we held a convention in the small village of Colomba, situated on the western slopes of the Santa Maria volcano located near Quetzaltenango. This area is called Colomba after the small town where the church is; it is the center of the coffee growing area of Guatemala, accessible only by a dirt road. But there was no problem in getting a good attendance because people came from all over the area where many worked in the coffee *fincas* and villages. Some walked, others came by bus and sometimes the *finca* owner allowed them to borrow a truck to provide transportation.

On Sunday afternoon there was suddenly great excitement in the whole town. One of the church members came running over to tell us that on his small radio he had heard that a revolution had just started. It was concentrated in the capital city where the rebels were trying to overthrow the government. The home where Esther and I lived was located in Guatemala City and also the seminary to where we had to return the team the next morning. Colomba is quite isolated, and we were not able to obtain any further reports, which increased our concern about the trip home because there might be sporadic fighting on the country roads. Often people took advantage of revolutions to stop cars and buses and hold up the occupants to steal and kill. On other occasions, they took advantage of the unrest and lack of police protection to get even with their enemies and innocent parties often became victims. The church in Colomba and the Evangelistic Team quickly decided we had better pray about the safety of the church members and for our safe return home. That was a very fervent prayer meeting.

We really prayed before setting off for home the next morning. There was no way to phone home or even contact the seminary to get reliable information on how the fighting was going. There are not many phones in the rural areas, which are mostly limited to government officials, and the lines are often cut by the revolutionaries to limit communication between the military units. The military takes control of the country and often the radio transmitters are taken over by them to promote their cause and to communicate with their bases and control the uprising. This time all radio stations were ordered to be repeater stations to the government station. So we felt our information was not entirely accurate. Once in a while a particularly successful revolutionary force took control of the radio stations so they could communicate their cause to the public. To find out just what was happening, we went to the local police, but they did not have any more information than what we had heard on the pastor's radio.

Prayerfully and very concerned we took off Monday morning. The dirt road up the hill to Quetzaltenango at 8,000 feet altitude was primitive and dangerous. But we arrived safely at this second largest city of Guatemala. There is a large military base there and of course, they had communication with the authorities in Guatemala City. We felt we could trust them and went to the base to find out about the progress of the fighting and the safety of the highland road to the capital city. In case we should not travel, we remembered that there is a large Presbyterian Church in Quetzaltenango and we had many friends where we could stay if we should not be able to go on home. A member of the congregation owned one of the bus companies to the capital and he also was able to give good counsel. We sent telegrams to Esther and to the seminary to let them know we were safe, where we were, and advised them of our plans. Telegrams were the most common way of communication those days, and everyone used them. Actually, it was not only the best but about the only way, as letters were often delayed for days or weeks. The telegram had a minimum of five words at three cents each, so the price was about 15 to 20 cents. We often combined words to stay within those five minimum words. This is easy in Spanish and all the missionaries were quite adept at forming meaningful messages that would be understood by our families and coworkers. They said, *We are in the city of Quetzaltenango and safe, see you tomorrow.* We were rather certain that they would be delivered to our home by bicycle from the central telegraph office in Guatemala City within a few hours.

After stopping at the telegraph office, we went to the military base to talk with the commander. Because I was a foreigner and missionary, we were received very courteously and the commander shared what information he had. He said that, so far the fighting was confined to Guatemala City and the surrounding area. He did warn us that the center of the fighting was at the new, still vacant, Roosevelt Hospital. It was named after our President Roosevelt because it was largely funded with friendly gifts from the USA. The revolutionaries had appropriated the empty buildings and felt well protected, but this created a grave problem for us. It was adjacent to the main highway and we had to pass very close to get to the center of town. Since the seminary was on the other side of town and the team lived in the dorm, we had to pass right close to the shooting. I was responsible for delivering the team to the director of the seminary and could not go home until they were safely in his hands.

The commander at the *cuartel* (headquarters) in Quetzaltenango told us he thought we would be safe and that there was no fighting reported along the highway or the three hour drive down the mountain to the capital city. So we took off after more prayer. The main road was mostly along Mayan villages and grazing or farming communities and there was seldom fighting in those areas. The commander thought we would be in no danger until we got near to the Capital City and the fighting at the hospital built alongside the highway.

He was right. We heard plenty of shooting, and heard the troops trying to take back the hospital buildings, but no shots came close to us. We got home safely, thanks to the Lord, who is always there to care for us when we need His help.

Miracle Gas Station
Southern Mexico, 1965

The dirt roads and potholes of the paved roads of Guatemala had taken their toll on our car and it needed a new set of tires. I mentioned to Esther one day that it sure would be nice to be able to buy the tires in the States. They were better tires and cost less than half the price of those in Guatemala. Why, we could visit Jean, Esther's sister in Fort Worth; now wouldn't that be a nice vacation? But that would mean two weeks of driving and only two weeks of vacation she said. But it wasn't long until she took me up on making the trip. When Charles and Vera Ainley heard about our plans, they wanted to go along and share the expenses. After getting our visas and permits, we took off. We would spend our month's vacation driving to Texas and back, a trip of six days driving each way.

After we got on the road, there were a few anxious moments when we worried if the smooth tires would make it, and each morning we carefully checked them for holes. On the road, we dodged every pothole we saw. So after crossing the border at Brownsville, Texas, the first thing we did was head for the tire store. The car was put up on the lift and the new tires chosen. A few moments later the attendant called me over to show me a big balloon on the inside of one of the front tires and said if we had gone another mile it would have burst. He added, "It would have blown out within a few more miles." Again, we thanked the Lord for caring for us and getting us safely to Texas.

We had a great visit with Jean, and the Ainleys spent their two weeks with Dr. and Mrs. Norman Taylor whom they had known in Mexico when they were stationed there. It was a good two weeks of vacation and mission was accomplished. We had a new set of tires and happily headed back home to Guatemala.

On the way home, we chose to go south from Brownsville, Texas, traveling along the eastern seacoast of Mexico. Traveling time through Mexico is about three days. It is a beautiful drive along the beaches and much cooler because of the ocean. The car had no air-conditioning and Southern Mexico is tropical, hot, and dry in the low country. The first major stop is Tampico, a major oil town, and the next stop is Vera Cruz, a beautiful beach city where we always planned to spend the night. Both are delightful places on the ocean. The next leg of the journey is from Vera Cruz south to Acayucan and this takes most of the day so we hoped to stay there. At Acayucan, one leaves the main highway to the Yucatán Peninsula and takes the road that crosses over the isthmus to the town of Tehuantepec, which is on the Pacific coast. From there it is a day's drive of about 250 miles to Tapachula and the Guatemalan border. So, when possible, we stayed all night in Tehuantepec because the accommodations are so much better.

Charles and Vera Ainley were well acquainted with Mexico having worked there many years as missionaries before being transferred to Guatemala and vetoed the eastern town of Acayucan and its poor accommodations. We got there late in the afternoon but we drove on. There is a nice motel in Tehuantepeque where we had stayed before and it was our unanimous decision that it was not too far even though we would have to drive after dark. Darkness is dangerous because of animals on the dark roads and there are many bad accidents, but I would be careful. The road across the isthmus in southern Mexico is about 135 miles and takes more than three hours. One leaves the eastern side of Mexico, which is somewhat populated, and drives into the low mountains of Chiapas and the sparsely populated tropics.

In our haste to get on our way, we forgot to buy gasoline in Acayucan. By the time I realized that we did not have enough in the tank to get all the way to Tehuantepeque it was dark and we were about an hour on our way. In the tropics, it gets dark with a bang. At six in the evening, it comes all at once, for there is no twilight. I pulled over to the side of the road and we talked it over. These uncertain times, when one has a hard time making a decision, is when you pray fervently for God's leading. We did just that, trying to choose the right thing, for a mistake now would be disastrous and maybe we would have to spend the night on a deserted road in southern Mexico. After a bit of looking at the map, Charles remembered that the little village of Matias Romero was about half way, but it was a small agricultural village and did not have a service station. But Charles was certain we could buy gasoline in an emergency from one of the truckers there. Several local residents transported produce to market every day and had their personal reserve hoarded away. The town is very isolated and about three miles off the highway on a dirt road, but that didn't seem to be an obstacle that could not be overcome. We were certain that some sympathetic soul would be willing to let us have a gallon or two out of his 50-gallon drum emergency supply. Even if they charged us double, it would make it possible for us to get to Tehuantepeque. Having decided to take that chance, we were on our way.

We drove on into the dark, and I watched the gas gauge very carefully. It seemed that we would never arrive at the little village. We did pass several turnoffs along the way, but none of them showed any lights or signs of a village. As the gauge got closer and closer to empty, we were all getting very nervous. This was very wild country and we had passed no one except a couple of donkeys and men on their way home from their farms. All of us were thinking, "What will we do if there is no gasoline?" That was when we came to a long descending hill and there in the distance was a nice big gas station all lighted up, right along the side of the highway. You can imagine the sighs of relief. I hurried to get there before they would turn off the lights and close for the night for we were just about the only car on the road. In a few minutes, we had filled the tank and were on our way.

Later that evening we arrived in Tehuantepeque and were welcomed to that lovely motel.

We had traveled that road at least six times before and there was no gas station or sign of one in the past. We have driven that road several times since, but there simply is no gas station there. We have searched and searched, and we even drove into the small village looking for it, but they told us there was no gasoline station in that area of Mexico. The country folks don't have cars and there is no need for a supplier. A couple of men have trucks to drive produce into market but they always buy their gasoline in Acayucan. There are not even any electric posts or electric lines to that spot. We have never again been able to locate that gas station. It simply does not exist. As we talked about it, our only conclusion was that it was a miracle. Had God provided a miracle just for us? Did God put it there to supply the needs of his negligent children? He often does just that. I don't know the answer. We didn't try to reason just how God did that miracle for us, but as we talked about it, we just thanked Him for His marvelous care.

How do you explain such a miracle on a country road, dark at night, and just a bit foreboding in the rural area of southern Mexico? You don't have to. In fact, if you could, you would lose much of the joy of watching God at work and think you did it yourself or could have done it if you had modern science at your disposal.

Esther Writes Home
About the Earthquake
Guatemala, February 4, 1976

A major earthquake hit us at 3:03 a.m. February 4, 1976. It registered 8.5 on the Richter scale. We were awakened by a violent shake and then it never seemed to stop. They tell us that it lasted for 39 seconds, but it seemed like an eternity. Esther wanted to run to the nearest doorway to be protected by the doorframe, but I held her in bed remembering that our apartment was fairly safe even with that big a jolt. (Maybe I was too afraid to do anything else). Running to a doorframe in the dark could mean falling over something or stepping on broken glass. After the shaking was over the next thing was to feel around on the floor to find the flashlight that had been knocked off the bedside table. I think I even asked Esther where she had left it. When we found it, we hurried outside where we joined the Thorps and other residents of the apartment buildings where we lived. It was very dark. All electric power had been cut off and there were no city lights anywhere. With my flashlight I checked the walls of the apartment building and found there were no serious cracks that would put us in danger, but we stayed outside until day break anyway.

At that moment, the Lord put it in my mind to see if we

could call home and let people know we were safe. Just maybe the phone would still be working. I went back into the house about 3:30 a.m. to phone daughter Phee and let her know we were all safe. We knew from experience that as soon as daylight came, the phone lines would be tied up and no one would be able to get a dial tone. (And that is just what happened. For almost a month it was impossible to get a line to the United States and the only communication was by ham radio.) Phee's phone rang, and after she woke up and got to the phone, we told her, "There has been a terrible earthquake but we and the Thorps are safe. Please call everyone in the family in the morning, including Esther's folks, and your brother and sisters and tell them we are okay, and then call Becky Thorp and tell her to call the Thorp family so that they will know we are all safe." It turned out that the phone communication was so bad after the quake that the Mission Headquarters in New York was not able to call any of the missionaries to find out if we were safe. For over two weeks, they could not find out anything about us and they were frantic.

Here is Esther's letter home written on February 18:

After experiencing most of the 800 shocks we have had in the past two weeks, we are almost getting used to the things. The only trouble is that we are never quite sure how strong the next one will be. There was an aftershock the next day of 6.2 that brought down what was left of the tower in the Cathedral. The earth was rather quiet then for about two days, just a few tremors; then at 4:00 this morning came another heavy one. For safety, John and I slept in the car for a couple of nights. I will confess that I was really scared! I know that your prayers have been a help to me. *I can take it now without that horrible sick feeling in my stomach every time the earth moves.* Sometime last week I knew that I could not go on being so frightened. I was no good to myself, or to anyone else. While reading my Bible for help God reminded me of the struggle that Jacob had with the Lord. I don't know if I struggled with God or He with me. Anyway, we had it out together, and He won and I am able to take it better now.

It seemed as though my part in this whole thing has been to stay home and take care of the visitors and there were many. Most of the hotels were destroyed or closed. I told you about

Dad's friend who was with us. He was so sure that things would be back to normal in a couple days that he flew to Tikal the next day, and because he insisted, Mrs. Hayter got him a taxi to Antigua on Friday, only two days after the earthquake. The road was blocked by landslides in several places, and the bulldozers had cleared some, and semi-leveled a passage over others. On that day, we had the heaviest quake since the first one, and he was on top of one of those landslides when it happened! Another slide started to come down the mountain. The driver had his wits about him, hit the throttle and got them out of the danger. When Melvin got to his hotel he found that the 18 guests were sleeping in the patio (this was not Hotel Antigua, but a native style building). The servants had prepared soup and *arroz con pollo* for the guests, but after that second big shake, they and the owner abandoned the place, and they were not seen again. So the guests had soup and *arroz con pollo* for supper, nothing else. The other guests had pulled a bed into the patio for Melvin with a shower curtain to cover him as protection against the dew. Next morning the guests prepared their own breakfast. Then one of them went out and found some taxis and they were very glad to get back to Guatemala City. There has been so much rubble in the streets, and so many quakes and tremors, that he had not been able to do any sightseeing. Melvin, who, you will remember, is an ex-navy man, said that he had never seen such destruction. Only in one town in Europe had he seen such terrible destruction by the bombing.

Well, he was glad to get out of Guatemala and left on Tuesday for Mexico. On Thursday, Don Weisbrod arrived and stayed with us. On Monday, he left for the north area of Guatemala to do relief work, and that afternoon the Sparks arrived. There is quite a bit of past history that I have not told you about. We visited them, and had invited them to come stay with us now. They will leave tomorrow, and Don will be back Friday. Last Thursday we had two members of Luis Palau's team here. Luis and another team member stayed with the Thorps. Luis and

team are here to make preparations for Billy Graham who will visit for a day. Mrs. Graham had a heart attack about a month ago, and they were vacationing in Acapulco at the home of a friend. Billy called Luis and asked him to make the arrangements for them to come down. So there was much to do. He is the royalty of evangelical circles, and I am sure that much the same type of preparations had to be made. Anyway, as soon as Billy, Ruth and Cliff Barrows arrived, people were ready for their visit. President Laugerud's representative met him, and took the party up in two helicopters for a two-hour ride over the devastated area, even landing at one badly damaged village. Billy had an interview with the President, who speaks rather good English. He told Billy that he had attended one of his campaigns in the United States. Finally, the Graham party reached the Ritz-Continental hotel where about 100 evangelical leaders were gathered to join them for a buffet luncheon. We had spent most of the morning at the airport because we were to be part of the reception party, and be in a press conference. But when the President calls, you drop everything and do what he says! After lunch all the pastors and anyone else who wanted to, went to the Central Presbyterian Church were Billy spoke to all of us. Bernice and I were to take care of Mrs. Graham so that she would not be too pressed by people wanting to meet her. We took her to the Pan American Hotel, and Bernice stayed with her, because I felt I had to go to a meeting that had been scheduled long before the earthquake. But no one came, just as I expected, and I was able to go back and have a good visit with Mrs. Graham. We compared notes on China. She is a very gracious person and Bernice and I were so pleased to be with her.

The town of El Progreso is being vacated so people are building shacks outside of town. Every building in town came down or was so badly damaged that it could not be used and will have to be bulldozed. The mission had just put up a new sanctuary for the Presbyterian Church and it was built out of pre-fab materials so is still standing. The city moved in and set up shop there. They even had one section divided off to be a jail. Did you realize that the Presbyterian Church has a jail? The government will level everything but the trees with a bull dozer. This will make the houses higher than the streets, which will help prevent drainage in the wet season. Now the people will be able to build more permanently. Wood and corrugated tin roofing are being saved as much as possible. The last day Don was there, he helped tear down the church school buildings which were of adobe and used what could be salvaged to put up some temporary shelter for the homeless. One of the homeless was a poor woman who had only a table under which to sleep. This general plan is being carried out by the government over the whole country where the adobe buildings have had to be demolished.

On Tuesday I went down to the church to work with the volunteers who were preparing small packages of the donated corn, rice, beans, sugar, and salt. Then one of the deacons and I took bags and blankets and went visiting. The pastor went in another direction, and another deacon to another zone. Of course, they have all been visiting and taking lots of food to families for the past two weeks, but it was my first time out. We only got four visits made. I was never hugged and kissed so much in one day! We were so grateful to find our friends still alive. The women appreciated our visit even though some of them had been visited before. We had to hear all about each one's experiences. We read Scripture and prayed with them. One woman had an affliction so she cannot talk. All she could do was to move her body, then put her hands together in an attitude of prayer and look up to heaven. That of course expressed what most of them told us. Neighbor helped neighbor. One woman is a nurse, and is helping those in her barrio who had been hurt. She, however, had done nothing to clean up her own house. It was still in disorder where the things had fallen. In another house, which was full of wide cracks, the lady sat calmly entertaining us. She had cleaned up everything, and only those cracks showed that there had been an earthquake. Of course, everyone was thanking God for having been saved.

One of the hardest things for me during all this was to know that there was no way we could advise Pep and Brad in Southern Africa that we are safe. We should have asked Phee to send them a telegram because all communication here is out and no one can get through. I was so sad that they had to send a telegram to Char to find out if we were okay. I wrote immediately, but don't know when mail service will begin. Cables of death notices were the only mail being accepted at the post office for a couple of weeks after the quake.

We love you all, and pray for you daily. Pray for dad. He has so many meetings, and sees so much of the damage and suffering it is beginning to get to him.

Love, Mother

Esther's General Report about the Earthquake
Guatemala, 1976

Thirty-nine seconds is a long time, long enough to kill over 27,000 people by falling adobe walls and unsupported roofs. Seven point nine on the Richter scale was strong enough to move our refrigerator 14 inches from the wall, and bring down chunks of masonry two meters square from church towers. As we see the wholesale destruction in the city, our hearts ache. Some streets are so filled with rubble that cars cannot get through. Whole blocks are leveled; others have only one or two damaged buildings still standing. This is multiplied over many times in the towns and villages east and west of the capital city. In the town of El Progreso the only usable building is the Presbyterian church and that is because the mission recently built them a structure supported with iron beams. For several weeks the church building housed the offices of the city hall, the Post Office and the jail. Imagine looking down your block and seeing no standing buildings where the day before it was completely filled with homes. Now there is nothing but rubble and some of your neighbors are buried under it. One lady told us that she thought that this must be the Second Coming, and she clapped her hands with joy and sat back to wait for Jesus to come. Another woman who lived alone saw that part of her roof had caved in and when she could not get out because her doors were jammed, she took up her Bible, sat in the middle of her room, and waited for the Lord to take her home. One thing for which we praise the Lord is that none of the missionaries were hurt. This is a true miracle, since many of them work in Indian villages where they have to live in adobe houses. In one case, a missionary couple jumped out of bed and stood against a wall, and the roof fell onto their bed. If they had not moved, they would have been killed. In another room of the same house, the people stayed in their beds, and the roof fell between the beds where they would have been standing had they gotten up.

We are as safe as anyone can be. The house we live in is built of reinforced poured concrete. Our large dining room window shattered, the kitchen cupboards opened, and the floor was littered with broken plates, bottles, glasses, and a few of my owl collection. But who is complaining! So many people who escaped with their lives had everything they owned buried under the rubble.

The first thing the missionaries did was to find out who needed help. The manager of the flour factory lives in our apartment building and when he told us he had lots of instant tortilla mix in 100 lb. sacks in the factory, we went right over and purchased a truck load so we could distribute it to our church members. It was then repackaged into small bags by the deacons so we could give them to those without any food. Those who are literally in the streets are living in make-to-do areas in the parks using blankets for a roof because their homes are demolished. But they did get a wood fire started in the street to toast their tortillas and make some coffee. We found people were helping and sharing with each other. Five boy cousins spent two hours the night of the quake rescuing a neighbor's maid who had been caught between two walls at the back of the house. The stated clerk of the Synod lives at the office building which is next door to a Catholic orphanage. His wife made a bonfire to keep her family warm, and all the orphans came over and gathered around. She made coffee for them all, and kept them and the Catholic sisters warm with their fire and hospitality. The people who live in Sanarate had their troubles, but when they heard that the folks in El Progreso were even worse off than they, the women cooked up a big pot of beans and made tortillas by the hundreds so the men could take the food over to them in trucks, even though they had to drive over badly damaged roads. This same generosity was repeated many times in many places.

You folks from the USA have been astoundingly generous. A US army field hospital was set up in the most seriously damaged area. Small planes and helicopters, landing on the highway, are constantly bringing in the wounded people from outlying settlements. Landslides have blocked most of the roads throughout the country and most bridges are down. Mexico sent in heavy equipment to help clear the roads. They also set up a portable kitchen with huge 200 gallon pots at our airport so helicopters could literally pick up the cooking pot and take the food hot to the villages. Plane loads of medicines, food, and clothing, as well as building materials, have been donated from the USA churches. It has been quite a big job for us to sort all of this and get it out to the people. We have been helping our church organize the deacons, working long days sorting the food and putting it in small bags getting it ready to deliver to our members. Relief organizations have brought in medical personnel to tend the wounded in the isolated areas.

The Guatemalan government has done a great job of relief operations. Within the hour, President Laugerud was out visiting the devastated areas. In the first week, he was everywhere, talking to the people in their Indian dialects and supervising the relief work. We felt great admiration and sympathy for him, for these were his children, in a way, and they looked to him for help.

The streets are filled with makeshift tents made of sheets, bedspreads, cardboard, and tin roofing. We saw one cardboard shack on whose wall was stamped, "Biltmore Hotel." Shanty towns have sprung up all over the city in the parks, on grassy dividers of streets, on sidewalks and any vacant lot. This is fine during the current dry season, but the rains will begin in a month or so and one wonders how they can find cover. Then, in response, several countries and individuals have offered to rebuild whole communities.

The Synod has an Emergency Committee which relates to the Committee of the Alliance of Evangelical Churches in Guatemala. This relief group handled supplies that are being distributed through the Presbyterian Committee, which in turn divides these things among the churches. In the Central and North Presbyteries, where the fault line lays, we have 28 churches destroyed, or needing major repairs. John is the head of the committee that is responsible for evaluation and restoring what we can with the funds that were sent by the Wichita Presbyterian Church. They canceled their building project to send us over $100,000 just to help us restore our church buildings. John was able to buy about 10 prefab warehouse structures here in the city, which make excellent church frames. They come with a locally made cement/asbestos roofing material and most villages now have, on their own, cleaned up the fallen adobe where their churches stood and are worshiping in the open air. They will put up the prefab structures and much later, when they have funds, will enclose them with walls and a facade according to their own liking. This way they will have their "own" church built according to their culture background. This way, we are not robbing them of taking their own initiative or making beggars of them, but giving them encouragement and a helping hand.

In the capital, the Colegio La Patria will cost more than $60,000 to restore. Mt Zion was not damaged at all. Our churches on the south coast were not as badly damaged. In the Quetzaltenango area many adobe buildings were damaged, but there was little loss of life. 15 manses are needing repair or replacement. None of our pastors were killed, and just a few of our church members were hurt or died. Over 500 Presbyterian church families have lost their homes. In North Presbytery, it is many times that because the towns are built right along the Motagua River Valley, which lies along the major fault. The government didn't even know it was there.

This disaster has unified the churches and the believers. Many people, whose faith had cooled, quickly came back to church. The first Sunday after the quake there was much rejoicing when we saw faces of those we thought were dead. Central Church could not meet in their building because of the damage, so they met outdoors in the patio of La Patria School.

There were many hugs and exclamations of "How glad I am to see you are alive and safe!" The churches have taken advantage of this scare and are giving out tracts and Bibles and talking to many about their spiritual relationship to God. An atheist whose life was spared said that he felt the presence of God during those awful 39 seconds, and came to the church to confess his faith publicly. One pastor was found digging in the ruins of a home. When asked where his children were, he answered that they were out visiting the neighbors and offering them help and speaking to them of spiritual things.

We are so grateful to God and you and for your prayers and generous gifts these days. God is using them greatly,

God bless you.

Esther and John Shackelford

CONCLUSION

Do We Like Being Missionaries?

Our first taste of being missionaries came in language school. The school was operated by the Presbyterian Mission and was located in Medellín, Colombia. During the week we spent four or five hours a day in class and then in the afternoons we went shopping so we could listen to people talk and try to use what we knew of the new language. Of course, the dictionary was close by. At meal times, we were encouraged to use our new Spanish vocabulary asking for the salt and pepper and trying to discuss the culture and people that were so new to us. They were long and tiring days.

After nine months of vigorous study, we flew to Barranquilla for our first Mission Meeting. It was quite a change in climate and in fellowship. We actually were among missionaries and discussing Mission business. Medellín has a very lovely climate, but Barranquilla was at sea level and very hot. What an introduction to our new assignment. At the mission meeting we were assigned to the Barranquilla Station where Esther would stay until April, when Peggy was due. Then we were to move to Cereté, many miles inland, where we were to encourage the rural pastors and church members and supervise the construction of a couple of small churches. A new health clinic in Nazarét was to be built so John got the job of that construction. He spent about three weeks of every month in these very rural areas of the Sinú Valley and then would come home for a week to have medical checkups and be with the family. The Sinú was full of malaria, diarrhea, and yellow jaundice so these checkups were urgent.

This portion of our letter home reporting on our first Christmas on the Mission Field tells it all:

February 19, 1947

Saludos Amigos,

You can never know how much your Christmas letters and cards meant to us unless you have been away from home and lonely during that family day. Thanks to your letters and prayers, the day was not as lonely as it might have been. We spent the day at the mission vacation house, located at the beach in Puerto Colombia, a simple rustic building with lots of open windows to catch any breeze from the ocean. We were able to get some Christmas carols on the short wave radio and that made us feel better.

Life is very interesting and much different. We are getting familiar with the way the older missionaries do things and learning a completely new set of social rules for this culture that extends to conversation at church, in the stores, and even on the streets.

The first trip into the jungle areas of the Sinú Valley, which is about three hours away by plane or a couple of days by road, was most interesting. We took the Mission Jeep and learned to sleep in hammocks and to swallow the new and definitely different food. The families are very poor, but still tried to give us something special even though they had to skimp for days after our visit to catch up. The wide rivers had no bridges, so there was a ferry called a *plataforma*. It was made of three dugout canoes tied together with planks on which the vehicles were driven. Power to cross the river was a cable tied upriver so a rudder against the current would move the ferry across. Once we had to rebuild a bridge over a small ravine in order get to the other side. The growth is so abundant that during the wet season no vehicle can travel, for the road is completely grown over and deep in swamp. We bathed by pouring water over our bodies with a dipper. We had to open over 100 gates which separated the huge cattle haciendas. One time I had to walk in front of the Jeep to look for stumps and rocks as there really was no road and the grass had grown up until we could not see the ground. This was a really new experience but richly blessed because we got to know the people and their sincerity and love for Jesus Christ and the Church. It is incredible how these folks got by so many miles from civilization.

After an all day trip in the Jeep, we would reach a little pueblo and it was so wonderful to have the people rush out to greet you with open arms. I don't know of any other time when I have been so warmly embraced. How it does humble one to think they consider the missionary so wonderful. You must pray that we will never let them down, but lead them always to a deeper life in Christ.

Imagine a family feeding you the best they have knowing they will have to eat less all week. Yet they are so happy to make the sacrifice just to have your visit. They can't even sit down at the outdoor pine table with you because they don't have enough plates, spoons and forks to provide for company. The food was a long way from our normal menu, but we felt we must eat it, even knowing that there was danger of amoeba and the resultant sickness. One really means it when praying, "Lord, bless this food to my body."

What a joy to be with these folks and learn to love them for they have come to know Jesus Christ in a very special way because of their poverty and isolation. In spite of all this, they are very generous in giving to the church and providing for a school teacher for the church school. We were to start the worship service at 10:00 a.m., but by 9:30 the grass hut church was full and many people were standing. Everybody was there so we just began early. What enthusiastic singing and vital testimonies of God's grace and love and we loved it!

We truly consider it an honor to be able to work with these people, and have already learned something of the power of God in this land. Sincerely, we feel that God is working and want you to know that He has already been answering your prayers for His blessings on Colombia, South America. We love being missionaries and thank God we can be here!

APPENDIX

John Meets God

Santa Barbara, California, 1935-1941

My new life in Christ really began on August 23, 1938 when I accepted Christ as my Savior. I was attending Santa Barbara State College. My roommates and I lived in a very small one-room house so we could afford to go to college. It had to be cheap and, believe me, it was. The house had an old dilapidated rocking chair that our landlord had provided as furniture for our so called *furnished* room. The accommodations consisted of a room large enough for three beds and this old discarded rocking chair. A lean-to had been added at the front which contained a sink, a gas burner, and a table with four chairs. It was screened in so we could use it as a kitchen and dining room, but it did get cold in winter. The bath was an add-on to the bedroom and would hold one person at a time. As I remember it, the rent was fifteen dollars a month and that included utilities, which consisted of a bare light bulb hanging from the ceiling. Each room had such a

bulb that you reached up to turn on and off. I guess the owner had never heard of wall switches. Not long after a breakfast of mush we each went our own way, so we didn't really need much of a house.

All summer I had been dating a girl who sang in the youth choir at the Presbyterian Church. There was a large group of college students in the church and most of them sang in the Youth Choir. Choir practice was one of our major youth activities. That summer I spent a lot of time with my date. God had used her to show me what the Christian life was really like and I wanted to learn more. The youth group enjoyed doing things together, but its activities could not be identified as any different from the non-Christian groups. However, being with this date and friend was different. She was spending the summer with one of her mother's friends but the summer would soon be over and she would go home, so we spent a lot of time together.

She came to our church because she wanted to be part of an active, vital group like she had in her hometown and wanted to continue in a Christian fellowship while in Santa Barbara. The Church in her hometown had taught her to pray, trust in the Lord, and live as though Jesus was a personal friend. I remember at Communion one Sunday how she remarked that she could almost feel God's very presence as she was meditating on the meaning of His death on the cross. This was new to me and I was deeply moved. The Holy Spirit had touched me through her and I was discovering that one could have a personal relationship with God. This impressed me deeply and was changing my thinking.

School started in the fall and one day I went back to our house between classes to study with no one around. I began thinking about what I was learning from my new experience with Christianity and from my girlfriend's mature attitude of the Christian life. As this change was taking place, a new life purpose was also developing for me — I began thinking about a reason for my life and I realized that I wanted the same kind of life she had. The Holy Spirit was speaking to me in a very special way. As I sat in that old rocking chair trying to memorize verb forms in a foreign language, I discovered a little booklet that this friend had put among my books. She had gone back home after the summer was over and I was lonely for her and our conversations about God and life. So when I found this little booklet it was much more interesting than trying to learn a new vocabulary. Since I had such a high regard for her and her lifestyle, I immediately read the booklet as though it was a message from her.

The little booklet was titled, *The Reason Why,* and had been written by Robert Laidlaw, a remarkable business man from New Zealand. Later on when Esther and I visited New Zealand as the International General Secretary for Christian Camping International, I discovered how important this man had been to the people there. One day when speaking to the executive committee of a camp near Wellington called El Rancho, I mentioned his name and the tract and how it had spoken to my need. This got an instant response, "Yes, we knew him and he was very influential in the development of this camp and other Christian programs." I found that Mr. Laidlaw was almost an idol of the Christian community in New Zealand.

As I studied the little booklet, I soon realized that I was not a Christian. As I read on, I discovered how God, as Creator of the universe, was Lord of all creation and that included me. It contained illustrations that brought me to recognize that there was no other way the universe could have come into existence except through God himself. The illustration he gave was that of a watch. "Do you think that the cogs, springs, and other workings of the delicate and complicated instrument just one day got together by coincidence and began to work in such a way that it could give the accurate time of day?" The author then directed my thinking into the relationship a person could have with such a Creator God and how Christ had provided a way for me to enter into close fellowship with the Creator of the world. Mr. Laidlaw quoted the Bible where it said that it was not by works nor by what man had been able to accomplish, but that in our carnal and sin-filled life there is no way to have *any* contact with such a Holy God. But in His great love and desire to have me become His friend and make me holy, He had died on the cross just for me! What a revelation! *God did this for me and I found He wanted to have a friendship with me!* I couldn't believe it, He wanted to be *my* friend! Of course, when the booklet suggested that I could move into such a relationship with the Omnipotent, Omniscient God, by simply desiring it and asking Him to come into my life, I said yes to Him! He accepted me as His child and son as I prayed right there and then, "Lord, forgive me for ignoring You and sinning against You. Please accept me as your child and give me that fellowship with You!"

That is when life really began, for I was now *born again, into a spiritual relationship.* As I sought to know Him, walk with Him, and talk with Him, I discovered what being His Child and a member of His household really meant. He soon gave me a new life, new friends and new friendships that have lasted all these years and whom I love and cherish.

Exciting Prayer Group on Campus

What a wonderful new life God had planned for me! Almost from the date of my new birth, God led me to a student prayer group on campus. It was a grass roots campus group which had not heard of InterVarsity or Campus Crusade. Those kinds of organizations were just getting started and had not yet spread to the Santa Barbara campus. In the fall of 1938, as a new Christian, I was subconsciously seeking a new life in Christ and new friends who had Christian perspectives, desires and recreation. Christians in this prayer group were a Godsend because they helped me develop a Christian philosophy for life and a new way of living. Second Corinthians 5:17 became the goal of my life, "Therefore if any man be in Christ, he is a new creature: old things are passed away; behold, all things are become new." (KJV)

When classes started in the fall, it was a little difficult to go back to live with my old roommate because I was no longer interested in the things he thought were important. The lifestyle he represented no longer appealed to me. We had rented a tiny two room house on Prospect Street that consisted of one room, a bath, and a kitchen. The kitchen was so small that by stretching out your arms you could touch the wall in either direction. I had met this roommate at the college group at the Presbyterian Church. We both sang in the youth choir. I had never shared his hedonistic lifestyle and thinking, but had tolerated his love affairs. Now I was turned off by it all. His main goal in life was to graduate and get a good job and all that went with it, but this definitely didn't fit into the way God was leading me.

I thank God that He led me to a new set of friends through the prayer group. It consisted of more or less 40 students who met in the little park adjacent to the campus to eat their sack lunches and discuss from a Christian perspective what was going on in their lives. They talked about how Christ was directing them in the little everyday things that happened on campus and they often referred to the Bible, looking for an answer to God's will for their lives and attitudes. We prayed for our friends and made plans for activities that would honor Jesus Christ. We hardly missed a day, for the weather in Santa Barbara seemed to be always in our favor — nice and sunny. We were not able to meet on campus but this was no problem since the park was adjacent to the campus. Even at that time, the state laws prohibited us from having prayer groups and Bible study meetings on campus. These new friends led me to love the Scriptures and seek in them how to live the Christian life. We prayed for each other, our relationships with others, and our special needs. Often we talked about friends that we wanted to accept Christ as Savior. We discussed how to avoid temptation and resolve our problems from Christ's point of view. This time together included a short study of a passage of the Bible led by one of the students. Sometimes Dr. Cyril Ross joined us and led the Bible study, explaining what the original Greek taught regarding the passage.

Dr. Ross was a retired Presbyterian Missionary from Korea and took me under his wing since I wanted to be a missionary. In my senior year, I still needed 15 hours of a foreign language to graduate. The college allowed him to tutor me in New Testament Greek for that whole year to fulfill the requirement of a foreign language. That special class was accepted for my language requirement at both college and seminary, so it paid double dividends. Dr. Ross became a very dear mentor and counselor to me as well as teacher. There was no doubt that God sent him to help me just when I needed him.

This prayer group was anxious to be active in sharing the Gospel and we formed a Gospel team that was invited to several small Churches in the area. One of the girls played the piano and others gave their testimonies or sang. Keith Pitman was a great soloist and I had a trumpet so when we spoke and sang in isolated places where there was no chapel or musical instrument we were able to entertain the folks. Once we drove over the hill to an isolated CCC camp, a program established by the government to give work and income during the depression. We talked to the guys at the camp, gave our testimonies and Keith sang. I didn't play the trumpet very well, but to them it was quite a novelty in that isolated area.

Keith became a very close friend and we often went on deputation together. In fact, the last year of college, we rented a tiny apartment with three bedrooms, and I was able to move from my old roommate into a home with Christian guys. This made it possible to move away from the old life and a roommate with whom I no longer had anything in common. By inviting three more Christian guys to come and live with us we were able to pay the rent. It took five of us to pay the monthly rent of twenty-five dollars. We were all so short of cash that five dollars each was just right for our budget. That price included utilities and furnishings. The owner of the apartment did not want to rent to college students, especially to fellows, because college men had a bad reputation for being rowdy. However, when I told her I was a ministerial student and would vouch for no big parties or drinking, she decided she would take a chance and let us rent it. Of course, we did not have a phone and we all had to walk to school, but it was not more than a couple of miles and we found a shortcut that went straight up the hill to the campus. The college was on a steep hill but we didn't mind the exercise and even made it on rainy days by putting on raincoats and hats. Once in a while, we were able to get rides home if the weather was too bad.

One evening the Gospel team was to meet to plan and pray for the weekend mission to speak at a church in Goleta. We would prepare our testimonies and practice the songs we were to sing. I objected, but Keith had accepted the invitation to go to the Church and was insistent that he and I join the others for the preparatory meeting.

"But," I said, "I don't have any gas in the car nor do I have any cash to buy any." He didn't have any money either. I was even planning to walk to school the next day because I didn't think I had enough gas to get home. But Keith was positive and said, "Let's go anyway and trust the Lord to get us home." So we went. Stepping out on faith was a new experience for me. I had never had any experience in that kind of trust so had not thought of that approach. The prayer group had a sponsor from the faculty at college who was a great Christian and was a Godsend to the group in more ways than one. He made contacts for us, represented us before the administration and gave maturity and stability to the group. He was at the prayer meeting/practice that night. After working out our plans for Sunday, we started for the door. That was when Professor Norman Taylor slipped his hand into my pocket and said, "The Lord told me you would need this." After we got outside, I felt in my pocket and there was a five-dollar bill! Money for gas to get us home *and* for the trip on Sunday evening and more. Gas was only twenty cents a gallon so it more than filled the tank. That was my first experience in seeing how God uses His children to provide for our needs and it opened up a totally new confidence in God.

During the last two years at college, God often did things that were miraculous in providing for me. I don't remember that there was a single time when I really worried about paying the bills; there always seemed to be just enough, and I never had to borrow to get by. This was during the depression and Mom and Dad were having a very tough time to keep from losing the farm so were not able to help us go to college. Mother did what she could by selling stockings to her friends at church and from her meager income, she bought me a new pair of shoes. She found out that I was putting cardboard into my old shoes every morning because they had large holes in the soles that were wearing out my socks. Often my sister Alma and I went back to Garden Grove for the weekend and Mom always gave us a liberal supply of home canned food to take back. Mom almost always fried a chicken to take back to share with my roommates. Before leaving, I often went out to the orchard and garden and picked some oranges and vegetables. Dad didn't have a lot of cash but was always generous with his garden so I was able to take back a good supply of food.

One semester when it came time to register for classes, I did have a real test of faith. It took us about three days to register, sign up for classes and work out our class schedules. The third day I ended up at the financial office. When the registration was finished at that last window, one had to have money in hand to pay registration, lab costs and tuition. I shared my dilemma with Keith and Bud and told them I would have to forego that semester because I didn't have any money. My thought was to take the semester off and work. That way I could save enough to be able to register and pay the tuition for the following semester. They suggested that we pray about it! What a lesson in trust; they taught me to pray and ask the Lord to provide for my needs. This idea was rather new to me, but I was willing to try and wanted to please them as well as the Lord. So at their urging we prayed. I then went back to school afraid to go to that window with empty pockets and the embarrassing moment when they asked for money. Would you believe it? That last day, I still didn't know what to do, for that afternoon I would have to pay the total. But I went ahead, signed up all morning then walked home to get a bite to eat for I had no money to buy anything at the school cafeteria. When I got home there was a letter from my sister Lucille that Keith had put on the table. I had not heard from her for a long time but she always had a word of encouragement for me. There in the letter was a check with enough to pay the entire registration for the full semester! I was alone in the house, and you can imagine the emotion when I realized that God had just answered our prayer and had provided just what I needed. Lucille was out of college and had a good job, but we had never discussed finances nor did she know of my struggles to register that semester. She simply had sent it because she felt the Lord moving her to do so. How great it was to discover the many ways God looks after us and to learn that I can trust Him to look after me. It taught me a valuable lesson in trust. It also gave me a good sermon for that weekend as our Gospel Team went out to minister. Can you guess what I preached about? It was on trusting God who cares for each one of us and delights in providing for our needs just as 1 Peter 5:7 says, "Cast all your care upon Him; for He careth for you." (KJV)

The contact with the prayer group led me to a serious study of the book of Romans. Virgil Hone invited me to a Bible study of a small group of college students that had found a Sunday School teacher willing to teach us. Joining that group started me studying the Word of God and was fundamental in establishing a solid faith. The book of Romans was fascinating and the beginning of a lifelong love for the Word of God. I had never heard of John Calvin or Martin Luther and now this new discovery of them and their works taught me to always go straight to the Book of Romans when a question or problem came up. I was a new believer and I needed this new foundation. All through seminary my mind took me back again and again to those basic concepts found in Romans and the theology and ethics of the Christian life laid out there by the Apostle Paul. What a marvelous place to start! God had it all planned and I just sat back and enjoyed every minute of it. At seminary when the opportunity came up to do an exegetical study of a book of the Bible in New Testament Greek it was only natural to choose Romans and how I loved studying it in the original language.

As God led me to this prayer group, He gave me life-lasting friendships and satisfied the longing in my heart for the *new life in Christ.*

Student Pastor at Summerland, 1939

After being accepted as a student for the ministry by the Presbytery of Santa Barbara, I was asked to be the student pastor at the Summerland Presbyterian Church under the leadership of the Reverend Dr. Bronson. The church was very small but this retired minister was anxious to help the congregation continue a testimony in Summerland. They needed someone to organize a

Vacation Bible School during the summer and work with the children during the school year. I was delighted to have this opportunity to begin my ministry. Summerland is near the college and Dr. Bronson was willing to give me twenty five dollars a month to pay my rent and food. The small financial help they offered took the place of the gardening jobs that I had worked at during the past few years. He never said so but I suspected that Dr. Bronson provided the funds out of his own pocket for the church had only a few members so their budget was very limited.

My first year as a Christian I attended the Presbyterian Church of Santa Barbara and they asked me to teach the junior high Bible class on Sundays and to lead the Christian Endeavor gang Sunday evenings. It was a great opportunity to begin sharing my faith and have an opportunity to be involved in ministry at the church, but when the Presbytery asked me to help in Summerland it was even that much better.

The summer daily Vacation Bible School was a great success. Dr. Bronson had obtained the local school building since the church had only a sanctuary and no Sunday school classrooms. A local resident who attended the church took most of the responsibility and through her contacts, many school children attended. After school, we would take the children down to the beach and have a picnic and a swim.

When winter came, I asked if we could have an evening meeting each week to invite the kids to a sort of club style group in the church. After consulting Boy Scouts and YMCA, we did our own thing but used the YMCA leadership manuals and story books. We had a good turnout and after pushing back some of the benches there was ample room to sit on the floor and tell stories about Christian heroes, and lead the kids in memorizing Bible verses. We helped them develop a desire to read the Bible and learn to pray. There was a good response and several made decisions for Christ and joined the church.

My most memorable and exciting opportunity was when Dr. Bronson asked me to preach on Sunday evenings. He was faithful and always came and was a great counsel to this neophyte pastor. This was my first time preaching a sermon. I prepared for weeks, and when the time came, I had to count on one of the girls in our prayer group at college to play the piano for us. I still remember the congregation that night. I brought three students from the prayer group and the leader of the VBS and her husband were there along with Dr. Bronson. I counted seven in the congregation! But the students sang well and one of them sang a solo. The only disappointing thing was that the sermon was way too long and dry. Sometime later Dr. Bronson told me that I didn't have to preach about everything I knew in just one sermon. But remember, I still had not had any classes in homiletics. They forgave me and still came back the next week!

Dr. Bronson was a great mentor for my first experience in directing the activities of a small church.

Missionary Kid in China
China, 1920 - 1938

At age 10, I [Esther] was sent off to a boarding school located in Tung Chow, China. In one of his letters to the family in the USA, my father John T. Bickford tells about the pain they all felt, as I had to leave home at such an early age:

I took Esther to Tung Chow on Wednesday afternoon on the train and helped her unpack and stayed overnight. I like it fine, and think it will do Esther a world of good. (There are no children to play with at the Mission Compound). On Friday, I hired an auto and took her mother out there to surprise Esther. There are 20 some girls and 30 boys, from the 6th grade through high school. She was pretty lonesome and could not keep her eyes dry when we left her this afternoon. During one of the talks we had, I talked to her about bearing a cross, telling her how suffering has to come, and we must bear it patiently and courageously for Jesus' sake and with His help.

After a later visit, Father writes the family:

She told me about her Bible studies in school and gave a very good account of Andrew the Apostle. There are only two others in her grade. One is a little Greek lad who is very bright but handicapped by a lack of knowledge of English; and the other is a big gawky American kid who is a smarty but not smart, at least that is the way I sized him up. Esther takes music which makes her practice every day. She did take Chinese, but the principal had her give it up as she was pressed for study time. She looks well, red cheeks & plump; her hair is about an inch long and is darker red than before. [She had radiation to remove scalp ring worm, which left her bald].

Another letter home tells of an outing with my parents:

On December 23, 1931 we made a trip to the Great Wall with Esther. We left Peitaiho at 6:15 a.m. and got back at 11:30 p.m. We had a 90 minute rail trip each way on the Chinese railway. We went on a two hour donkey ride from the depot up into the mountains to a famous cave temple. On the way, we climbed up to a tower on the Great Wall, where we saw one of the fighting towers at close range. It was about 30 ft. square, with windows to fight from and a stone stairway to the roof. It was in pretty good shape for having stood 2,000 years. We returned by way of Shan Hai Kuan (Mountain Sea gate) and hired rickshaws to take us down to the ocean. There we saw the end of the Great Wall, a British fort, the British summer camp, and ate supper at the canteen. We were fortunate in getting a ride back to the depot with some guards on their little rail road car, drawn by mules. Then we had a tedious wait at the depot, but that was the only unpleasant thing of the day. Esther told her mother there was "quite a nice-faced god in one temple, but the one beside it, oh, it was simply terribly ugly."

A letter written from Shuntehfu in January 1931 reports:

We are keeping Esther home this term and not sending her back to Tung Chow. She was sick twice in four months and again at Christmas time so her mother decided she would teach her at home. It is hard on Margaret, but we hope to have her catch up on her studies and build her up physically. I had to take a trip to Peking to get her. I spent all night and all day getting to Peking. The next morning at nine, we were safely reposing on the train coming home, which we reached at ten in the evening. [Missionaries had to take the third class coach to save money and in China it was not the cleanest or the most elegant].

China was not a pleasant tourist haven with Biltmore hotels in those days. Clothing had to come from the USA, ordered from the Montgomery Ward catalog. The order was shipped by boat and took months. Some food and most of the clothing had to be ordered up to six months ahead. But God was present even in the toughest times.

College in the United States

I graduated from North China American High School in Tungchow in June 1937. My parents felt I would profit from another year in the Orient so I did post-high school for one year at the Pyongyang Foreign School in Korea where I graduated in 1938. Ruth Graham attended the same school a few years later. When Ruth was in Guatemala we had a great time comparing notes about the school. After graduation, I sailed to the United States to live with my father's sister while I attended Santa Monica Junior College in California.

"Wow, after that long ocean voyage I am in the States! Auntie was at the Long Beach harbor to welcome me and has made room for me in her lovely home in Pacific Palisades. It will be nice to live here and now I can go to Santa Monica Junior College, which is nearby."

My folks would be home from China after I graduated and I would go live with them in Highland Park during their furlough. They wanted me to go to Occidental College and I agreed. I graduated from Junior College in 1940 and roomed with my cousin Patty Millar while we attended Occidental College. We had the most fun together and I was glad to have an opportunity to get to know my cousin as we had been separated all that time except when I was on furlough. I earned a Bachelor of Arts Degree from Occidental in 1942 where I also earned a teaching degree and minored in music. I graduated from San Francisco Theological Seminary with a master's degree in Christian Education in 1944.

During the summer, I was able to get work at Zephyr Point, the Presbyterian Conference Grounds at Lake Tahoe. I waited on tables, worked in the kitchen and did various odd jobs as a member of the staff. It was a very special time for me because one evening at the camp fire we were challenged to consider giving our lives to the mission field. That was it! God spoke to me very clearly that evening and when they invited us to come forward to dedicate ourselves to becoming missionaries, I went forward and confirmed what I had always thought was a great calling. My parents had helped me to see the importance of taking the Gospel to people in other parts of the world and I was ready. Of course, my mind was on China. I had spoken Chinese as a child and still remembered, although studying Spanish in college had overshadowed much of my vocabulary. This decision motivated me to think maybe I would do just as mother had done, go to seminary and marry a missionary.

He Loves Me

Esther's Story
San Francisco, California, 1942

I had to have a job at seminary to help pay my bills. Just about all the students had to work and the administration gave us jobs on the campus that would otherwise have to be done with outside help. I was lucky; they assigned me to be the librarian, which meant that I sat at the desk every evening to answer questions and check out books. When I was not busy, I had time to study while on the job. It was a neat job and I loved it.

All the students ate in the dining room, which is located in the basement of the men's dorm building, right next to Montgomery Hall which housed the library and class room building. But the women had their dorms at the bottom of the hill in an old mansion that had been renovated to house us. We had to walk up and down the hill several times a day.

One evening a handsome fellow came by to ask about the section where books on sermons where stored. After that first encounter, I noticed that he came in almost every night and spent the evening in that section. Later I discovered that he was the student pastor at Weed, California where he preached two sermons every week, and was looking for good themes, material, and illustrations. He seemed to be very busy getting his studying done as well as preparing for the weekends. Every evening he stopped by the desk to check out some books and soon we became good friends as we took time to chat.

One night as we talked, he commented that it was a very dark night outside and that it was late. Wouldn't I like him to walk me down the hill to the women's dorm? Well, it was a bit late and I felt safer with a man to walk me home, so I accepted. This good thing soon turned into a habit and I found I looked forward to those evening walks especially when it was moonlight! One evening we stopped at one of the benches along the path, and before I knew it, he was kissing me. Before going to seminary, I was dating a fellow from the college department of the Highland Park Church where we lived while I went to Oxy. I was saddened by the bad news from the war department saying that he had gone into the air force and was shot down somewhere in the Pacific. I will admit I was a bit lonely and John's comfort and kiss was just what I needed. It wasn't long before that happened every night as we walked down the hill.

Then we discovered that we both had made commitments to be missionaries. Something new was happening. I couldn't go home for the summer because my family was in China, so I took a job at Lake Tahoe working for the Presbyterian Conference Grounds. One night when the speaker asked if there were any of us that felt called to be missionaries, God moved me deeply and I went forward at the campfire and accepted the call to go to the mission field. John told me that he had heard Dr. Sam Higgenbottom at Synod Meeting while he was in college, and after that message he too felt that God was calling him to be a missionary. But of all places, he wanted to go to India. I had grown up on the mission field in China and was thinking of going back to China. I knew the language pretty well and was familiar with the customs so it was a natural.

These differences brought on a lot of discussion, but one night he said to me, "I think we should be married and go to the mission field." I was bothered by the lack of a very romantic proposal, but that was soon taken care of when he told me *he dearly loved me! Of course I said yes!*

It didn't take him long to buy me a beautiful ring and the next step was to make the formal announcement to the other students. There was a ritual involved and custom dictated that we announce our engagement at dinner. We told Harlow Willard, the dining room host, of our plans. He said he would prepare a special evening meal so we could tell everyone. He set it all up and made the arrangements. Later he sent us a bill for the cost of the cake. Harlow was a very dear friend of John's and later he became the best man at our wedding. I had reserved the place of maid of honor for Patty, my cousin and best friend.

At dinner, everyone seemed to know what was going on. Maybe it was because we had been spending so much time together on the campus and were seen walking off into the moonlight every evening. The time came for the announcement and Harlow set us up. We stood and kissed and told everyone the good news. We also emphasized that we were planning to go to the mission field together which brought a great applause.

We both graduated in May, 1944 and our wedding was set for the end of the summer on August 3rd. Mother and Daddy had not met John, but my glowing reports on his life and ministry as a student pastor helped them give their approval and permission. I am sure that our planning to go to the mission field cinched their willingness to have him as a son-in-law for they had been missionaries for many years. We spent our honeymoon at Mount Hermon where Dwight and Ruth Small and Harlow and Claire Willard were vacationing. They had been our best friends in seminary and we had great times together. After vacation, we headed north to the church in Weed, where I became the *Lady of the Manse*.

John and I served as Pastor and Lady of the Manse for two years. That ended when a telegram came telling us that we had been appointed by the Board of Foreign Missions of the Presbyterian Church to go to Colombia, South America. We resigned from the church, and after going home to Highland Park where Esther's parents lived to pack, we were on our way.

About the Editor

Phee Paradise was blessed to be a missionary kid and loves to share that experience in her writing. She has contributed to several books, including *A **Ruby** **Christmas*** and *A **Dozen** **Apologies***, both available on Kindle.

She prays that her work will be used by God to His glory. You can read some of Phee's stories at <u>FaithWriters</u>.

L-R: Janet, Phee (Phyllis), Charlotte, Fred, Pep (Peggy), Esther, John

Look for other books

published by

Pix-N-Pens

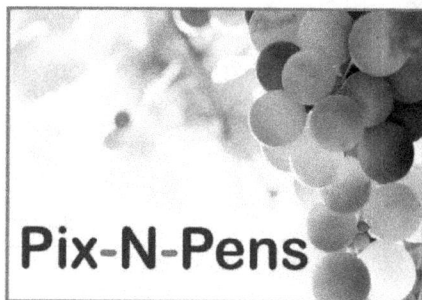

Pix-N-Pens Publishing

www.PixNPens.com

and

Write Integrity Press

www.WriteIntegrity.com

www.ingramcontent.com/pod-product-compliance
Lightning Source LLC
Chambersburg PA
CBHW062047270326
41931CB00013B/2980